rhiannon lawrence

EAT FREE

no gluten. no sugar. no guilt.

······ rhiannon lawrence ········

EAT FREE

no gluten. no sugar. no guilt.

BONNEVILLE BOOKS
SPRINGVILLE, UTAH

ISBN 13: 978-1-59955-465-5

Published by Bonneville Books, an imprint of Cedar Fort, Inc., 2373 W. 700 S., Springville, UT 84663
Distributed by Cedar Fort, Inc. www.cedarfort.com

LIBRARY OF CONGRESS CATALOGING-IN-PUBLICATION DATA

Lawrence, Rhiannon.
  Eat free : no gluten, no sugar, no guilt / Rhiannon Lawrence.
    p. cm.
  ISBN 978-1-59955-465-5
  1. Gluten-free diet--Recipes. 2. Sugar-free diet--Recipes. 3. Cookbooks.
  I. Title.
  RM237.86.L39 2010
  641.5'638--dc22

  2010033010

Design by Danie Romrell
Cover design © 2011 by Lyle Mortimer
Typeset by Danie Romrell
Edited by Megan E. Welton

Printed in China

10 9 8 7 6 5 4 3 2 1

Printed on acid-free paper

To Jeff, Cam, Ben, and Zari—

Without you, life wouldn't be as sweet.

rhiannon lawrence

Honeyville
FARMS

BLANCHED
ALMOND FLOUR

"I prefer Honeyville blanched almond flour to any other almond flour. Honeyville's blanched almond flour is very fine, which works wonderfully in all of my delicious gluten-free recipes."

-Rhiannon Lawrence

Rancho Cucamonga, CA
9175 Milliken Ave.
Rancho Cucamonga, CA 91730
(909) 243-1050

Brigham City, UT
1080 North Main St. - STE 101
Brigham City, UT 84302
(435) 494-4193

Salt Lake City, UT
635 N. Billy Mitchell Rd.
Salt Lake City, UT 84116
(801) 972-2168

Chandler, AZ
33 South 56th St. - STE 1
Chandler, AZ 85226
(480) 785-5210

Find this and many other delicious Gluten-Free products at:
www.honeyvillegrain.com
or
www.honeyvillef...

Madhava Agave
The sweet and simple choice

Madhava Agave Nectar is an all-natural sugar replacement made from the succulent juice of the Weber Blue Agave plant. It's a simple plant based food that is a healthy alternative to highly processed sugar and artificial sweeteners. Our Agave Nectar is certified USDA Organic, vegan, kosher and gluten-free.

Madhava Agave Nectar comes in two shades of sweetness: light and amber.

Our Light Agave is mild and pleasant; it adds sweetness without flavor making it a perfect substitute for any dish where sugar is normally used.

Our Amber Agave has a subtle maple-like flavor making it a delicious addition to baked goods, barbecue sauce, roasted meats and many other dishes.

- Great Tasting
- Sweeter than Sugar
- Low Glycemic Index
- Natural Inulin
- Free of Common Allergens

USDA ORGANIC

MADHAVA
AGAVE NECTAR
www.madhavasagave.com

rhiannon lawrence

Beverages, continued

Entrees

Soups

Delectable Desserts—The Holy Grail of Gluten-Free Sugar-Free Cooking

Cakes and Desserts

Cookies

Toppings

About the Author

TO INSPIRE OTHERS to start on the path of health and wellness is rewarding. To visit flavors, colors, textures and the aroma of new experiences in food is set out on an adventure. We are a culture destined to find a better way to live through sharing. It is my pleasure to be a part of this sharing adventure through food.

As a registered dietitian and college professor, I believe knowledge is power when it is sweetened naturally with a pinch of ingenuity and good intention. For years, it has been my quest to help others understand the benefits of eating delicious, real, health-giving food.

The recipes contained in this book are based on those principles of knowledge, ingenuity, and good intention punctuated with natural sweetness. Rhiannon's time-tested recipes are simple to prepare, delicious to experience, and healing to both mind and body.

Throughout our years as friends, Rhiannon has introduced me to her immutable talent of finding the best of what life has to offer. This book offers readers a glimpse into a way of life that respects the natural goodness of all things including food.

Recently a student stopped me after class to tell me that her entire outlook on life had changed in such profound, positive ways as a result of choosing to learn about and eat foods that were respectful to her body. She, in turn, attained more self-respect than she had ever experienced up to this point in life.

It is with great courage and love that we bring ourselves, our families, and our communities to higher ground. It is with this same courage and love that Rhiannon brings this book into the hands of those who want to change the way we feed ourselves and those we care about. Food is about family. Food is about culture. I invite you to experience the tastes, aromas, colors, and feel of delicious and nutritious culinary adventures in the following pages.

Rachel Jones, MPH, RD
Nutrition Dept.
University of Utah

Introduction

I'VE ALWAYS considered myself a "health nut." I shop at health food stores and eat organic. I am a member of a great CSA (community supported agriculture), which means I pay for weekly shares of a community farm, and I'm aware of my food's carbon footprint. I ate organic throughout my entire pregnancy. I made my own baby food, and I drive my family nuts with little health tips and supplement/vitamin info. Apparently, all this wasn't enough.

Enough for what? I'm not obsessive. I'm not into health fads or weight loss diets. My bottom line is that I feel better when I eat well. Interestingly enough, my definition of "well" changed in September 2009.

I need to back up a bit here. My intention with this book is to share how I changed my lifestyle—not to give the world another weight-loss book. All of my recipes are gluten free and sugar free. Some of my recipes are vegan, some vegetarian, and some are downright carnivorous. All are delicious. I believe that diet is a component of lifestyle. It is important to me that my diet supports my active lifestyle.

After having my baby in 2008, I struggled with hormonal imbalance, weight gain, and depression; basically, I was miserable and did not feel like myself. I was as active as I had been before I delivered my baby and was eating what I considered a healthy diet. At this point, I began working with a brilliant hormone doctor named Dr. Uzzi Reiss. Dr. Reiss did a battery of tests (saliva, urine, and blood) and determined several things. In addition to having hormone issues, I was pre-diabetic and had gluten sensitivities.

These diagnoses came as a shock to me and meant that I needed to get really clear about what gluten was and why it was to be avoided. Gluten is a substance present in cereal grains—especially wheat—that is responsible for the elastic texture of dough. A mixture of two proteins, it causes illness in people with celiac disease. It is considered an inflammatory protein even in people without sensitivities.

Dr. Reiss explained that he was most concerned with my pre-disposition to diabetes (my Hawaiian grandmother, who has passed away, had diabetes, and Polynesians in general are genetically pre-disposed to diabetes). If I continued eating the way I had been, there was a pretty good chance I would have diabetes by age forty. Yikes! No thanks!

Incidentally, I also have a stepson that has been diagnosed with ADD. My husband and I had researched natural treatments for ADD in addition to prescription medications. We worked with my stepson's teachers, tried a couple of different medications, and decided that we'd switch the whole family's diet. We limited dairy and cut out sugar and gluten entirely. The change in diet seemed to have the most impact. We've taken our son off of his medication and manage his ADD with diet, exercise, and environmental support.

I enrolled in a nutrition class at the University of Utah, and I researched everywhere I could for gluten-free and sugar-free recipes. I explored wonderful blogs, websites, and cookbooks from dedicated cooks who specialized in celiac and diabetic diets. I was inspired to create gluten-free and sugar-free alternatives to family-favorite recipes. In addition to being gluten free and sugar free, I wanted recipes that were nutritious, packed with protein, and tasted really, really good.

But before I could do this, I had a few beliefs about food that I needed to address. I love baking. Baking is meditative to me. It's a way for me to connect with myself on an almost spiritual level and a way for me to show love. I'm talking real baking—nothing from a mix: homemade pies, cookies, cakes, breads, and so forth, all from scratch. White refined flour and sugar were staples in my home. I didn't bake every day, but I probably averaged a sweet sugary confection at least once a week. My stuff was good too. I have friends who still dream about my strawberry rhubarb pie.

So the big challenge I faced was how to make these same dishes without gluten or sugar. Other big factors were taste and overall satisfaction. I'm the main cook at my house. I'm big on family dinner each night, brunch on the weekends, and lots of special traditional holiday foods. I needed food that tasted great to both me and my family because I certainly wasn't about to prepare multiple meals.

I started off with the gluten-free products available at natural food stores. In my opinion, they tasted like processed food with a really strange texture and no flavor. I can't lie to my taste buds. My mouth knows what a pizza crust, a cookie, and a bagel are supposed to taste like. I'm not going to pretend

introduction

that those gluten-free mixes and frozen entrees are delicious. Edible? Kind of. Delicious? Not even close. Most gluten-free items that I found at the grocery store or health food store were made with rice flour, potato starch, or mixes of various starchy flours without wheat.

I wanted to try something outrageous here. I didn't merely want to eliminate gluten. I wanted to cut out starch completely, add protein and fiber, and maintain taste and texture. This was a crazy thought when I considered what was available at natural food stores. I wanted to make meals and treats that my gluten-tolerant friends would crave in addition to replacements for people living with celiac disease and sugar restrictions alike.

Then I discovered almond flour, coconut flour, quinoa flour, garbanzo bean flour, white bean flour, and so many other flours without grains or starch. My favorite is almond flour, and I use it for all my cooking and baking and in the recipes throughout this cookbook. I love the added fiber, protein, and subtle nutty flavor. I really hope you will too!

This cookbook is an introduction to healthy eating options. All of my recipes are simple; you don't have to be a chef to make them. Your entire family will love them, and I doubt anyone will even notice that they are lacking gluten or sugar. I use whole foods and organic products. I believe we truly are what we eat, and we should place a great value on where our food comes from and what is in it.

Remember, these recipes are meant to be enjoyed immediately. There are no preservatives, so these dishes won't keep as long as other preserved, gluten-filled, and sugared options.

Try one. Try them all. I hope you enjoy them as much as my friends and family do.

Rhiannon Lawrence

Recommended Products & Ingredients:

Almond flour—I use Honeyville Grain's blanched almond flour. This is the best almond flour I've found. It's fine in texture and works well in baking. Not all almond flour is created equally! Some brands are a bit too coarse and will not yield optimal results.

www.honeyvillegrain.com

Agave—Agave is a natural alternative sweetener. I like agave because of its glycemic index. The glycemic index, or GI, ranks carbohydrates according to their effect on our blood glucose levels. Madhava certified organic agave has a GI of 32. Refined sugar has a GI of 64. Stevia has a GI of 1. I use certified organic agave and stevia in my recipes.

http://www.madhavasagave.com

Stevia—A natural herbal sweetener, stevia is available in fine powder or liquid form. I use both agave and stevia in my recipes. I've found that stevia doesn't taste the same as agave in some of my recipes; I use agave for most of my baking.

Dark chocolate—I love chocolate. The darker the better, in my opinion. Dark chocolate is full of anti-oxidants that fight free radicals, and chocolate is a great source of magnesium. Milk chocolate contains more sugar and milk, so I avoid it altogether. I use a variety of chocolate products for baking. I love Ghirardelli dark chocolate chips, which range from 60 to 72 percent cocoa.

Vanilla—I use organic vanilla in my baking. You can purchase organic vanilla extract (not imitation vanilla) at health food stores or online.

Dried Fruit—I use fruit juice–sweetened dried fruit in place of sugar and cane sugar–sweetened dried fruit. Juice–sweetened dried fruit is available at most health food stores, Whole Foods, or online.

Fresh fruit and veggies—I always use organic produce. I don't want chemicals or pesticides in my food. Some of my recipes use the rind of various citrus fruits. It is very important that these be organic! The rind of citrus fruit is where most chemicals reside in fruit that has been sprayed. I also use a veggie wash.

Meat—I use some free-range ground turkey and chicken or grass-fed lamb. I also love wild fish and frequent my local fish market.

Eggs—I use free-range organic chicken eggs.

Oil/butter—I use organic butter in some recipes, I use grapeseed oil in other recipes, and I use extra virgin olive oil in a few recipes. Grapeseed oil is a great alternative to butter and can be used to make vegan recipes. It is a polyunsaturated affordable oil that is light in color and flavor. I mostly use extra virgin olive oil as a finishing oil because I love the flavor it adds to some dishes.

Disclaimer: While agave is a natural sweetener, and while it has a lower glycemic index than refined white sugar, it is still a sweetener and contains calories. Sweeteners should be used sparingly. My recipes are part of a healthy diet. But as always, all health concerns should be addressed with your personal physician.

recommended ingredients

BREAKFAST, BRUNCH, AND ALL THINGS EGGS

Chili Relleno Bake

My family and I love Mexican food. We love chilies and use them a lot. This is a fun spin on chili rellenos.
I like to serve this for brunch with fresh pinto beans and a salsa bar.

- 1 lb. grated Monterey Jack cheese
- 1 lb. grated cheddar cheese
- 2 (4-oz.) cans green chilies, drained and seeded
- 4 egg whites
- 4 egg yolks
- ⅔ cup milk
- 1 tsp. sea salt
- Fresh ground black pepper
- 1 tsp. Honeyville blanched almond flour

Preheat oven to 350 degrees.

Spread half of grated cheese, mixing both the Monterey Jack and Cheddar cheeses, in a well-buttered 2-quart baking dish. Spread seeded green chilies on top of cheese. Cover with remaining grated cheese.

In a small bowl, beat egg whites until stiff and set aside. In a separate bowl, beat together egg yolks, milk, salt, pepper, and almond flour. Fold in egg whites to yolk mixture.

Pour egg mixture over green chilies, using a fork to allow egg to ooze through cheese. Bake at 350 degrees for 30 minutes. Add sliced tomatoes around edges and bake for 20 more minutes.

Slice and serve!

Coconut Custard

Coconut custard is my brother Elijah's favorite food, and my mother made it for my brother's birthday every year as a special treat. I wanted to create a healthy alternative to this family favorite. Coconut is high in fiber and very nutritious. This recipe is an incredibly decadent addition to brunch or works as a fantastic dessert. I love to top it with assorted fresh berries!

Preheat oven to 350 degrees.

Mix agave, eggs, milk, vanilla, and almond flour in a blender. Add melted butter and blend. Be sure not to add melted butter before blending eggs or eggs will cook prematurely.

Pour custard mixture into bowl and stir in unsweetened coconut. Pour custard into buttered pie pan and bake at 350 degrees for 1 hour or until a metal knife inserted near the center comes out clean.

Allow custard to cool completely, which can take several hours. Chill cooled custard in refrigerator until ready to serve, up to 72 hours. Top with fresh berries to serve.

- ½ cup Madhava organic light agave
- 4 eggs
- 2 cups milk (light coconut milk adds extra coconut flavor and is really delicious)
- 1 tsp. vanilla
- ½ cup Honeyville blanched almond flour
- ½ stick melted butter
- ½ cup unsweetened coconut
- Fresh berries for topping (optional)

German Pancake with Almond Flour

This German pancake was a special treat in my house growing up. My mom would make this on holidays and birthdays. I wanted to share this memory—sans the white flour—with my kids. They love their pancake topped with 100 percent natural maple syrup. I love it topped with fresh berries!

- ¼ cup butter
- 1 cup Honeyville blanched almond flour
- 1 cup milk
- 6 eggs
- 1 tsp. vanilla
- Dash of sea salt
- 100% pure maple syrup (optional)
- Fresh berries (optional)

Preheat oven to 375 degrees.

Place butter in a large glass casserole dish or divide it between two 9-inch round pie dishes. Place dish in preheating oven to melt butter, removing the dish(es) as soon as butter has melted. Careful, the dish(es) will be hot.

Blend remaining ingredients in a blender for about 30 seconds or until whipped. Pour batter into baking dish(es) and immediately place in hot oven. Bake at 375 degrees for 30–45 minutes or until edges are lightly browned.

Remove from oven and serve hot, topped with some lemon juice and fresh berries or 100 percent natural maple syrup.

Mad Greek Frittata

I like to use high-quality, organic, locally grown ingredients in all of my cooking. I buy my sun dried tomatoes, olives, artichoke hearts, and cheeses from a great little Italian market.

Preheat oven to 375 degrees.

Sauté tomatoes, olives, and artichoke hearts in oven-safe skillet over medium-high heat until warmed through, 2–3 minutes.

In medium bowl, whip together eggs and add fresh ground black pepper. Pour over tomato-olive-artichoke mixture. Sprinkle feta crumbles on top of egg mixture. Bake at 375 degrees for 15–20 minutes or until eggs are springy when touched with a spatula or fork.

Slide a spatula under frittata to remove from skillet or turn over skillet onto serving platter. Slice into wedges and enjoy!

- ½ cup sun dried tomatoes in oil, chopped
- ¼ cup pitted kalamata olives, chopped
- ½ cup artichoke hearts in oil, chopped
- 5–10 eggs, depending on size of oven-safe skillet. Small skillets: 5–7 eggs. Large skillets: 8–10 eggs.
- Fresh ground black pepper
- ⅓ cup feta cheese

Margarita Frittata

Margarita pizza is what I think of when I think of Italy. This light frittata works as a good substitute for me.
I love making this in the summer when fresh garden tomatoes and basil are in season.
Feel free to add other fresh veggies for a great Italian-flavor veggie frittata.

- 2 Tbsp. butter or oil (extra virgin olive oil or grapeseed oil)
- 1 organic tomato, diced
- 5–10 eggs, depending on size of oven-safe skillet. Small skillets: 5–7 eggs. Large skillets: 8–10 eggs.
- ¼ cup chopped fresh basil
- ⅓ cup Parmesan cheese grated
- Fresh ground black pepper

Preheat oven to 375 degrees

Heat butter or oil over medium-high heat in oven-safe skillet and sauté tomatoes until warmed but not softened.

In medium bowl, whip together eggs, basil, Parmesan, and fresh ground black pepper. Pour egg mixture over sautéed tomatoes. Bake at 375 for 15–20 minutes or until eggs are springy when touched with a spatula or fork.

Slide a spatula under frittata to remove from skillet or turn over skillet onto serving platter. Slice into wedges and enjoy!

Ham and Cheese Frittata

Frittatas are great served warm or at room temperature, making them the perfect food for brunch, lunch, or even a light dinner with a side green salad!

- 2 Tbsp. butter or oil (extra virgin olive oil or grapeseed oil)
- 1 small potato, washed and diced into small cubes
- ½ cup ham, turkey ham, or other nitrate-free meat sliced into small cubes
- 5–10 eggs, depending on size of oven-safe skillet. Small skillets: 5–7 eggs. Large skillets: 8–10 eggs.
- ¼ cup fresh chives, chopped
- ⅓ cup Parmesan cheese, grated
- ⅓ cup cheddar cheese, grated or cubed
- Sea salt
- Fresh ground black pepper

Preheat oven to 375 degrees.

Heat butter or oil in an oven-safe skillet and sauté potatoes over medium-high heat for 5–8 minutes. Potatoes should be browned and softened. Add meat and sauté until warmed through.

In medium bowl whip together eggs, chopped fresh chives, grated Parmesan, salt, and fresh ground black pepper. Pour mixture over sautéed potatoes and ham. Drop in cheddar cheese so that you have chunks of cheese throughout your frittata. Bake at 375 degrees for 15–20 minutes or until eggs are cooked through. Frittata will be springy when touched with a spatula or fork.

Slide a spatula under frittata to remove from skillet or turn over skillet onto serving platter. Slice into wedges and enjoy!

Veggie Frittata

Veggie Frittata, or "Clean Out the Fridge" Frittata, is an easy go-to meal at my house. I frequently make this dish with whatever veggies, herbs, and cheeses I have on hand.

- Tbsp. butter or oil (extra virgin olive oil or grapeseed oil)
- 1 zucchini, diced
- 1 small shallot, diced
- ⅓ cup diced asparagus
- ½ cup sliced mushrooms
- ⅓ cup diced peppers (I love a bunch of color in my frittatas, so whatever peppers you have will work great!)
- 1 tomato, diced
- ¼ cup chopped fresh chives, or other fresh herbs
- ⅓ cup Parmesan cheese grated
- Fresh ground black pepper
- 5–10 eggs, depending on size of oven-safe skillet. Small skillets: 5–7 eggs. Large skillets: 8–10 eggs.

Preheat oven to 375 degrees.

Heat butter or oil over medium-high heat in oven-safe skillet. Sauté veggies for 3–5 minutes until cooked through but not soggy. Add tomato and stir just until warmed but not softened.

In medium bowl, whisk together eggs, chives, Parmesan, and fresh ground black pepper. Pour mixture over sautéed tomatoes. Bake at 375 for 15–20 minutes or until eggs are springy when touched with a spatula or fork.

Slide a spatula under frittata to remove from skillet or turn over skillet onto serving platter. Slice into wedges and enjoy!

eat free

Asparagus Frittata

Asparagus is a super food. It is high in folic acid and is a great source of many vitamins.
Not only is asparagus nutritious, but it's also one of my favorite vegetables.
This asparagus frittata is an easy way to work in some of this fantastic green food!

- 2 Tbsp. butter or olive oil
- 1 cup asparagus, washed and cut into 1-inch pieces, trimming off hard ends
- 5–10 eggs, depending on size of oven-safe skillet. Small skillets: 5–7 eggs. Large skillets: 8–10 eggs.
- Sea salt
- Fresh ground black pepper
- ½ cup grated Emmentaler cheese (this is a really yummy hard Swiss cheese. Regular Swiss or Gruyère work too.)

Preheat oven to 375 degrees.

Heat butter or oil over medium-high heat in oven-safe skillet. Add asparagus and heat until cooked but still firm, 3–5 minutes. A fork should slide through easily, but asparagus should not be mushy.

In medium bowl, whip together eggs. Add sea salt, fresh ground black pepper, and grated cheese. Pour egg mixture over asparagus in skillet. Bake at 375 for 15–20 minutes or until eggs are springy when touched with a spatula or fork.

Slide a spatula under frittata to remove from skillet or turn over skillet onto serving platter. Slice into wedges and enjoy!

Basic Cheese Omelet

My boys love cheese and eggs, so naturally my basic cheese omelet is a family staple. I like my kids to have protein at breakfast, and this is a great way to make sure they do.

- 2–3 eggs per omelet
- Sea salt
- Fresh ground black pepper
- ½ tsp. chopped fresh chives, basil, or oregano (optional)
- 1 Tbsp. butter or oil
- ½ cup mixed shredded cheddar, swiss, and havarti (or substitute your favorite cheese)

Whisk together eggs, sea salt, fresh ground black pepper, and fresh herbs. Set aside.

Heat butter or oil in small frying pan, taking care not to burn butter. Pour egg mixture into frying pan and cook until almost cooked through and tops of eggs are slightly runny.

Place shredded cheese on half of omelet and fold egg over and cook for another minute until cheese melts.

Garnish with fresh salsa, chopped herbs, or enjoy all by itself!

Spinach Omelet

I love omelets. I especially love the flavors of this omelet. Spinach is full of nutrients and is a great source of iron. I was anemic and needed extra iron during my pregnancy, so I ate this omelet almost every day while I was pregnant!

- 2–3 eggs per omelet
- ¼ tsp. fresh-squeezed lemon juice (concentrate will not work)
- Sea salt
- Fresh ground black pepper
- 2 Tbsp. butter or your choice oil, divided in half. (I like the flavor of butter best, and I love the flavor of truffle butter when I can find it.)
- ½ cup mushrooms, washed and diced
- 1 cup fresh spinach, washed
- 1 Tbsp. cream cheese (optional)
- ½ tomato, diced
- 1 Tbsp. chopped fresh dill
- Twist of lemon

Whisk eggs until yolk and whites are nicely whipped. Add lemon juice, sea salt, and fresh ground black pepper. Whisk together and set aside.

Melt 1 tablespoon butter or heat oil in small skillet over medium-high heat.

Add mushrooms to skillet and sauté just until they give up their juice, 3–5 minutes. Lightly salt and pepper mushrooms and set aside in a bowl. Sauté spinach in skillet until wilted and significantly reduced in size. Set aside.

In separate bowl, heat cream cheese to soften, add sautéed mushrooms, diced tomatoes, and freshly chopped dill. Set aside.

Add remaining butter or oil to skillet and heat. Pour egg mixture into skillet and cook until egg is almost set—the top will be a bit runny. Top with cream cheese mixture and sautéed spinach on one half of the omelet. Fold egg over to cover filling and cook for a minute longer to heat filling through.

Garnish with more chopped dill and lemon twist.

Quiche Lorraine

I use my potpie crust for my quiche crust. You can spice it up by adding any extra herbs you have—fresh rosemary and chives are some of my favorites! You can also add your favorite veggies to the filling to make a fabulous tart for any meal.

Crust:
- 1¾ cups Honeyville blanched almond flour
- ½ cup grated hard cheese (I use Manchego, but Parmesan works great too)
- ½ tsp. sea salt
- 4 Tbsp. unsalted butter, cold and cut into small pieces
- 1 egg

Filling:
- 10 slices nitrate-free bacon
- ½ cup shredded Swiss cheese
- ¼ cup minced shallot
- 4 eggs, beaten
- 1 cup light cream or milk
- 1 tsp. salt
- ¼ tsp. Madhava organic agave
- Dash of cayenne pepper

Preheat oven to 350 degrees.

Combine all crust ingredients in food processor and pulse until they form a ball. Press dough into tart or pie pan. Bake at 350 for 12–15 minutes or until lightly browned and remove from oven.

While crust bakes, fry bacon in large skillet over medium-high heat until crisp. Drain on paper towels and then chop into small pieces.

In a medium bowl, combine bacon, Swiss cheese, and minced shallot, and pour mixture into quiche crust, spreading evenly. In a separate bowl, whisk together eggs, cream, salt, agave, and cayenne pepper, and pour mixture over bacon, cheese, and shallot mixture in crust.

Bake quiche at 350 degrees for 20–25 minutes or until fork inserted in the middle comes out clean. Let cool for 10 minutes before serving.

Spinach and Feta Quiche

Spinach is a great source of iron and nutrients. It's packed full of flavor and is a green veggie that I use all the time.

Crust:
- 1¾ cups Honeyville blanched almond flour
- ½ cup grated hard cheese (I use Manchego, but Parmesan works great too.)
- ½ tsp. sea salt
- 4 Tbsp. unsalted butter, cold and cut into small pieces
- 1 egg

Filling:
- 1 cup thawed, drained, and packed spinach
- ¼ cup minced shallot
- ¼ cup sun-dried tomato, chopped
- ½ cup feta cheese crumbles
- 4 eggs, beaten
- 1 cup light cream or milk
- 1 tsp. salt
- Fresh ground black pepper

Preheat oven to 350 degrees.

Combine all crust ingredients in food processor and pulse until they form a ball. Press dough into tart or pie pan. Bake at 350 for 12–15 minutes or until lightly browned and remove from oven.

While crust is baking, mix spinach, shallot, sun-dried tomatoes, and feta crumbles. Spread evenly into baked crust. Whisk together eggs, cream, salt, and pepper and pour over spinach mixture.

Bake quiche at 350 degrees for 20–25 minutes or until fork inserted in the middle comes out clean. Let cool for 10 minutes before serving.

rhiannon lawrence

Tomato Egg Cups

I'm always looking for fun and easy ideas for dinner. This is a great one for summer when you have an abundance of fresh garden tomatoes. Tomato Egg Cups are delicious with chicken on a bed of steamed spinach or for breakfast with gluten-free toast.

- 4 large tomatoes, washed
- 4 eggs
- Sea salt
- Fresh ground black pepper
- ½ cup shredded cheese (I like Monterey Jack, or a hard Italian cheese, like Parmesan.)

Preheat oven to 425 degrees.

Cut the tops off the tomatoes and scoop out the seeds. Fill each tomato with one egg. Sprinkle with salt and pepper and top with shredded cheese.

Place tomatoes on a foil-lined baking dish and bake at 425 degrees for 20 minutes for "dippy," or runny, soft eggs.

Banana Chocolate Chip Muffins

My mother is famous for her banana bread and banana chocolate chip muffins. I wanted to create a low glycemic version of this homey treat that was nutrient packed and still delicious. Almond flour adds fiber and protein, Greek yogurt adds protein, bananas are a great source of potassium, and dark chocolate is a great source of magnesium.

- 2 cups Honeyville blanched almond flour
- ½ tsp. baking soda
- ½ tsp. sea salt
- Dash cinnamon
- Dash cloves
- ½ cup grapeseed oil
- ½ cup Madhava organic agave
- 2 eggs
- ½ cup Greek yogurt
- 2 ripe bananas, mashed
- 1 tsp. vanilla
- ½ cup Ghirardelli gourmet 72% cacao baking chocolate chips

Preheat oven to 350 degrees. Line a muffin tin with 12 paper liners OR grease and flour a 5 x 8-inch bread pan using almond flour.

In a medium mixing bowl, combine almond flour, soda, sea salt, cinnamon, and cloves and set aside. In a stand mixer or using a hand mixer, combine oil and agave.

Combine eggs, Greek yogurt, mashed bananas, and vanilla and mix well. Slowly add dry ingredients to wet ingredients, mixing well. Fold in dark chocolate chips. Pour batter into prepared muffin tin, filling each liner two-thirds full, or into prepared bread pan. Bake at 350 degrees for 15–20 minutes for muffins or 30–35 minutes for bread. Muffins and bread will be lightly brown, and a toothpick inserted in the center will come out clean when they are done.

Lemon Poppy Seed Muffins

My son Cameron asked me to reinvent this recipe. He loves lemon poppy seed muffins and was so excited that I made this version just for him.

- 2 cups Honeyville blanched almond flour
- ½ tsp. baking soda
- ½ tsp. sea salt
- ½ cup grapeseed oil
- ½ cup Madhava organic agave
- 2 eggs
- 1 tsp. vanilla
- ½ tsp. almond extract
- ½ cup Greek yogurt
- 1 tsp. lemon rind
- 1 Tbsp. poppy seeds

Preheat oven to 350 degrees. Line a muffin tin with 12 paper liners OR grease and flour a 5 x 8-inch bread pan using almond flour.

In a medium mixing bowl, combine almond flour, soda, and salt. Set aside.

Using an electric mixer or wire whisk, combine grapeseed oil, agave, and eggs. Mix well. Add in vanilla and almond extract. Add Greek yogurt and mix well for 1–2 minutes. Mix in lemon rind and poppy seeds.

Slowly add dry ingredients into wet ingredients, mixing well. Pour batter into paper-lined muffin tin, filling halfway, or greased and floured 5 x 8-inch bread pan. Bake muffins at 350 degrees for 20–25 minutes for muffins or 30–35 minutes for bread. Muffins and bread will be lightly brown, and a toothpick inserted in the center will come out clean when they are done. Cool on a wire rack and enjoy!

Zucchini Muffins

Some of my favorite childhood memories include eating zucchini muffins and zucchini bread. My mother made the most delicious muffins with garden fresh zucchini. This recipe is a spin on the old family favorite but without flour or sugar, and I think you'll find them just as tasty. I can't keep these muffins in my house—they fly off the counter the minute they come out of the oven! Zucchini is full of fiber, folate, potassium, vitamin C, and vitamin A, making it a staple veggie in my house.

- 2 cups Honeyville blanched almond flour
- ½ tsp. sea salt
- ½ tsp. baking soda
- 1½ tsp. cinnamon
- ½ cup grapeseed oil
- ½ cup Madhava organic agave
- 2 eggs
- 1 Tbsp. vanilla
- ½ cup shredded zucchini, peel included
- ½ cup toasted pecans or walnuts (optional)

Preheat oven to 350 degrees. Line a muffin tin with 12 paper liners OR grease and flour a 5 x 8-inch bread pan using almond flour.

In a medium bowl, combine almond flour, sea salt, soda, and cinnamon. In a separate medium mixing bowl, using an electric mixer or wire whisk, combine grapeseed oil, agave, eggs, and vanilla, mixing well. Add zucchini to wet ingredients.

Slowly add dry ingredients to wet ingredients, mixing well. Fold in nuts, if desired. Pour muffin batter into prepared muffin tins, filling each liner halfway, or fill greased and floured bread pan two-thirds full. Bake at 350 degrees for 12–15 minutes for muffins, or 30–35 minutes for bread. Muffins and bread will be lightly brown and a toothpick inserted in the center will come out clean when they are done.

Orange Cranberry Muffins

These delectable morsels are perfect for cold fall mornings. I like to use apple juice–sweetened dried cranberries instead of sugar-sweetened dried cranberries. You can find fruit juice–sweetened dried fruit at health food stores. Frozen cranberries will add tang instead of sweetness for an alternative cranberry muffin.

- ½ cup grapeseed oil
- ½ cup Madhava organic agave
- 2 eggs
- ½ cup Greek yogurt
- 1 Tbsp. vanilla
- 1 Tbsp. orange zest*
- ½ tsp. baking soda
- ½ tsp. sea salt
- 2 cups Honeyville blanched almond flour
- ½ cup juice-sweetened dried cranberries OR frozen cranberries for more tang

*I use organic fruit, especially when I'm using the rind of citrus fruit. Chemicals and pesticides reside in the rind and don't belong in my baking!

Preheat oven to 350 degrees. Line a muffin tin with 12 paper liners OR grease and flour a 5 x 8-inch bread pan with almond flour.

In a large mixing bowl, using an electric mixer or wire whisk, mix grapeseed oil, agave, and eggs. Add Greek yogurt, vanilla, and orange zest. In a separate mixing bowl, combine soda, sea salt, and almond flour.

Slowly add dry ingredients to wet ingredients, mixing well. Fold in cranberries. Pour muffin batter into prepared muffin tins, filling each liner halfway or floured bread pan two-thirds full. Bake at 350 degrees for 20–25 minutes for muffins or 30–35 minutes for bread. Muffins and bread will be brown, and a toothpick inserted in the center will come out clean when they are done. Enjoy!

SIDES AND SALADS

Arugula Salad with Lemon Vinaigrette

Arugula is rich in calcium, vitamin A, vitamin C, iron, and other nutrients. It's a superstar green veggie and a good lettuce for salads. I love the peppery flavor of raw arugula and find that it pairs really well with a lemon vinaigrette. This salad is crisp and delicious on its own and goes great with my Chicken Parmesan Strips (see page 59) for a complete meal.

In small bowl, whisk together olive oil, sea salt, pepper, lemon juice, and agave for vinaigrette and set aside.

In serving bowl, toss toasted pine nuts with arugula. Drizzle lemon vinaigrette over salad, mixing thoroughly to coat salad evenly.

Serve immediately and enjoy!

- 2 Tbsp. olive oil
- ¼ tsp sea salt
- Fresh ground black pepper
- ¼ cup lemon juice from fresh lemons
- 2 Tbsp. Madhava organic agave
- 1 (5-oz.) package arugula
- ¼ cup toasted pine nuts

Avocado Mango Salad

Avocados are a great source of monounsaturated fats, vitamin E, and folate. Avocado was one of my daughter's first foods and remains one of her favorite foods to date. I sneak them in everywhere! I love the bright color of this salad and find that avocados and mangos are such a treat together!

- ½ cup sliced almonds
- 1 ripe mango
- 2 ripe avocados
- ¼ cup diced green onions
- 6 cups of mixed greens
- 4 Tbsp. olive oil
- 1 Tbsp. balsamic vinegar
- Sea salt
- Fresh ground black pepper

Toast sliced almonds for 2–3 minutes under broiler, watching carefully to prevent burning. Remove from oven when almonds are lightly browned and set aside to cool.

Dice mango and avocado into ½-inch cubes and thinly slice green onions. Cut mixed greens into bite-size pieces.

Toss together greens, avocado, onions, and mango in large serving bowl and top with toasted almonds.

In small, separate bowl, whisk together olive oil, balsamic vinegar, sea salt, and fresh ground black pepper. Pour dressing over salad and toss to coat.

Enjoy!

Black Bean Fiesta Salad

This is my go-to salad for barbecues and family parties. It's great served with gluten-free chips or on its own. The leftovers also taste great over eggs the next morning! Beans are full of prebiotics, which aid in digestion, and the peppers are a great source of vitamin C. All around, this is a nutrient-packed salad.

- 1 can black beans, rinsed
- 1 cup corn, fresh or frozen
- 3 peppers, diced (red, orange, yellow, green, or purple)
- 1 large or 2 small avocados, cut into small cubes
- 1 large ripe tomato, diced
- ½ cup chopped cilantro, plus extra for garnish
- Juice from 1–2 limes (for flavor and to prevent browning), plus extra for garnish
- Sea salt
- Fresh ground black pepper
- 2 Tbsp. Italian seasoning

Rinse black beans in colander and place in large mixing bowl. Add corn to beans. Wash, deseed, and dice peppers and tomatoes into similar sized pieces and add to beans and corn. Add cilantro, lime juice, and Italian seasoning and mix well. Season salad with sea salt and fresh ground black pepper to taste. Chill in refrigerator for a minimum of one hour to allow flavors to combine. Garnish with fresh cilantro and lime wedges. Enjoy!

Green Goddess Chicken Salad

Green Goddess is such a great dressing with a ton of depth and flavor. I love fresh dressings—they are simple to make and don't contain any preservatives or unnecessary ingredients. This one is especially tasty and is great on any number of veggies.

Dressing:

- 2 anchovies packed in oil, drained
- 1 small garlic clove
- ½ cup packed flat-leaf parsley
- ¼ cup packed basil
- 1 Tbsp. oregano leaves
- 1 Tbsp. fresh baby dill
- ¾ cup natural mayo (I use Lemonaise Light)
- 2½ Tbsp. fresh lemon juice (juice from 1 large lemon)
- 2 Tbsp. snipped chives
- Sea salt
- Fresh ground black pepper

Salad:

- 2 large tomatoes, cut into large chunks
- 1 (9.8-oz) jar piquillo peppers, drained and chopped
- 3 inner celery ribs with leaves, thinly sliced
- ½ cup kalamata olives, pitted and coarsely chopped
- 1 (5-oz.) package baby spring mix or your favorite greens
- 5 cups chicken—I use an organic rotisserie chicken and pull the meat into bite size pieces (shrimp or tempeh work great too)

Dressing

In a food processor or blender, pulse anchovies, garlic, and herbs (I use a mini food processor that is perfect for sauces). Add mayo and lemon juice and process until smooth. Pour into small mixing bowl and fold in chives. Season with salt and pepper.

Salad

Pull chicken into bite-sized pieces and let cool to room temperature. In a large bowl, mix the tomatoes, peppers, celery, olives, and salad greens. Add cooled chicken. Add dressing and toss to coat.

Strawberry Summer Salad

I love fresh, juicy strawberries at the peak of summer. They are so flavorful, and they complement spinach salad perfectly. This salad is great as a side or delicious with grilled chicken for a complete meal.

Toast pine nuts on baking dish under the broiler for 1–2 minutes, watching carefully so they don't burn. Set aside and let cool.

Combine fresh lemon juice, agave, and olive oil in small mixing bowl. Whisk together to emulsify. Season with sea salt and pepper to taste. Set dressing aside.

Wash spinach and chop into bite-sized pieces. Wash strawberries, remove stems, and slice into bite-sized pieces. Combine spinach and strawberries. Break up goat cheese into bite-sized pieces and fold into spinach and strawberry mixture. Add cooled toasted pine nuts. Add dressing and toss to coat.

Dressing:
- ¼ cup lemon juice
- 2 Tbsp. Madhava organic agave
- 2 Tbsp. olive oil
- Sea salt
- Fresh ground black pepper

Salad:
- ½ cup toasted pine nuts
- 5 oz. spinach, washed and dried
- 1 cup sliced strawberries
- 3 to 4 oz. goat cheese

Yogurt Fruit Salad

This is a lighter version of fruit salad that I used to have as a kid. Instead of whipped topping, this salad is made with vanilla yogurt. This is flavor packed and such a treat that I made it every day when I was pregnant.

- 1 apple, peeled and diced
- 1 pear, peeled and diced
- 1 nectarine, washed and diced
- ½ cup blackberries, washed and halved
- ½ cup strawberries, washed and sliced
- ½ cup blueberries, washed
- 1 banana, diced
- 1 (32-oz.) container organic low-fat or fat-free vanilla yogurt
- Juice from 1 orange

Wash and chop fruit into same-size pieces. Combine chopped fruit, yogurt, and orange juice in large mixing bowl, coating fruit evenly.

Pour salad into serving bowl, garnish with orange rind or a sprig of mint, and refrigerate until ready to serve.

Basic Basil Pesto

I love pesto in the summer. I make it fresh weekly and use it on meats, seafood, veggies, and all by itself. I serve pesto as an appetizer with gluten-free rice crackers and raw veggies. It's fantastic! You can also freeze pesto in ice cube trays to pull out during those fall and winter months when you're craving the taste of summer. I will vary the ingredients depending on what I have available, but here's my basic basil pesto recipe.

- ½ cup toasted raw almonds (I like almonds instead of pine nuts, but really any nuts will do)
- 1 cup fresh basil leaves, washed
- ½ cup grated Parmesan cheese
- lemon—just a squirt
- 2 cloves of garlic
- Sea salt
- Fresh ground black pepper
- Olive oil

Place raw almonds on baking sheet and broil in oven for 2–3 minutes until browned but not burned. Remove from oven and let cool. Once cool, pulse toasted almonds in food processor until coarsely ground. Add basil, Parmesan, squirt of lemon, and garlic to a food processor and pulse to desired consistency. Add salt and pepper to taste and slowly drizzle olive oil in processor until desired consistency is reached.

Pesto will keep in the refrigerator for up to one week. Pesto is a great go-to snack with veggies and rice crackers. Enjoy!

Garden Fresh Salsa

The key to good salsa is fresh ingredients. I use organic local garden tomatoes, peppers, and onions. I vary the ingredients depending on what comes out of the garden. Any blend of tomatoes, peppers, and onions works great! This salsa is best the second day so the flavors have had a chance to meld. I love this with chips, mixed with mashed avocado for guacamole, or over eggs in the morning. Enjoy!

- 1 large green pepper, finely diced
- ½ white or yellow onion, finely diced
- 1 bunch cilantro, washed with stems removed and chopped
- 5–6 large tomatoes, finely diced
- 1 habenero pepper, minced (Habeneros pack a lot of heat. You might want to try a small portion of the pepper and then adjust for your desired level of heat. I use one whole habenero to give my salsa quite a kick!)
- Fresh lime juice
- Sea salt

I dice my veggies into same sized pieces, except for the habenero pepper, which you want that as small as you can get. You may want to wear plastic or latex gloves when handling hot peppers, as the oils from the peppers can stay on your skin and may burn. Mix ingredients in a large bowl, add fresh lime juice, and salt to taste.

Another option is run all ingredients in a blender of food processor for a smooth salsa. Both options are great. It's up to you how chunky you want your salsa.

Hummus

Hummus is a staple at my house. My kids love hummus as a snack; I love it on gluten-free wraps with veggies and chicken; and we serve it often at parties. Hummus is packed with flavor, protein, fiber, and prebiotics.

- 2 (8-oz.) cans garbanzo beans, drained, with ¼ cup bean liquid set aside
- 1 cup tahini
- Juice of 3 lemons
- 2 cloves garlic
- ½ tsp. ground fresh cumin
- Dash of cayenne pepper
- 1 tsp. sea salt
- 2 Tbsp. olive oil plus extra for garnish

Drain garbanzo beans and save ¼ cup liquid. In a food processor, blend together garbanzo beans, garbanzo liquid, tahini, lemon juice, garlic, and 2 tablespoons olive oil. Pour into serving bowl.

Make small indentation in the middle of hummus, pour olive oil in center, and sprinkle with ground cumin, cayenne pepper, and sea salt for garnish. Serve with carrots, cucumbers, and jicama, and enjoy!

Roasted Stuffed Chilies

Another summer favorite of mine are stuffed roasted chilies. These are great with eggs in the morning, alongside grilled chicken or lean steak, or fantastic by themselves! I like to mix things up with different cheese combinations. My favorite is probably smoked Gouda and Monterey Jack. Try a few and see what you like the best!

- 4 large Anaheim chilies
- 4 slices smoked Gouda (or shredded Gouda)
- 4 slices Monterery Jack (or shredded Monterey Jack)

Preheat oven to 400 degrees.

Wash chilies and remove stems. Slice each chili in half lengthwise and scrape out seeds. Stuff each chili with either shredded or sliced cheese until each chili is almost overflowing. Secure each chili with a toothpick.

Line cookie sheet with foil.

Arrange stuffed chilies, cheese side up, on cookie sheet and roast at 400 degrees for 20 minutes or until chili skin starts to bubble and blacken and cheese is nice and bubbly.

Spinach Artichoke Dip

Artichokes are a great source of potassium. I love their flavor and try to use them whenever I can. This is a fun and easy dip to serve with veggies or gluten-free crackers. This is a quick go-to for parties!

- 2 to 3 cloves garlic, minced
- 1 Tbsp. olive oil
- 1 (12-oz.) package frozen spinach, thawed
- ½ (12-oz.) package frozen artichoke hearts, thawed and chopped into small pieces (if frozen artichokes aren't available I use 3 to 4 artichoke hearts chopped into small pieces)
- ½ cup milk or cream
- ¾ cup shredded Parmesan cheese
- Sea salt
- Fresh ground black pepper

In medium saucepan over medium-high heat, sauté garlic in olive oil until lightly browned. Add spinach and artichoke hearts. Once spinach and artichokes are warmed through, add milk or cream and shredded Parmesan, stirring constantly until thickened. Remove from heat and season with sea salt and pepper to taste. Serve warm.

BEVERAGES

Chocolate Peanut Butter Shake

I started making protein shakes for my son so that he would get more protein in his diet and to sneak in the occasional fruit and green veggie. This recipe is by far the favorite and can be made with any kind of protein powder or milk. We like protein sweetened with stevia and skim milk or almond milk. We also use natural peanut butter, which is peanut butter that lists only peanuts on the ingredients.

- 1 scoop chocolate protein
- 1 banana, fresh or frozen
- 1 heaping Tbsp. all-natural peanut butter
- 1 handful spinach or kale (optional)
- 1 cup milk
- 2 cups ice

Blend thoroughly in blender and enjoy!

Peach Raspberry Shake

When making fruit smoothies and shakes, I like to use my own organic fruit that is either fresh or that I have frozen myself. Not all store-bought frozen fruits are gluten free. I advise using fruit where you know its source.

- 1 scoop vanilla protein
- ½ cup frozen raspberries
- ½ cup frozen peaches
- 1 handful spinach or kale (optional)
- 1 cup milk
- 2 cups ice

Blend thoroughly in blender and enjoy!

Kefir Smoothie

Kefir is like yogurt. It's a great source of probiotics and can be dairy free. You can use coconut kefir and almond milk to make a diary-free smoothie that is delicious and nutrient packed. This is one of my favorites and a great way to sneak probiotics into my kids' diet.

- ½ cup plain kefir
- 1 banana
- ¼ cup blueberries
- ¼ cup raspberries
- 1 handful spinach or kale (optional)
- 1 cup milk
- 2 cups ice

Blend thoroughly in blender and enjoy!

Mango Strawberry Delight

My kids love to get mango smoothies from the local smoothie shop. I don't love the sugar content of these smoothies, so I made a healthier version that has the same flavor and packs a punch of nutrition as well. I sneak in kefir to add probiotics and spinach or kale to add iron and other nutrients. I'm more likely to get my kids to drink a mango smoothie than to eat a handful of spinach, so I consider this a win-win!

- ½ cup plain kefir
- ½ cup frozen mango chunks
- ½ cup frozen strawberries
- 1 handful spinach or kale (optional)
- 1 cup milk
- 2 cups ice

Blend thoroughly in blender and enjoy!

Tropical Smoothie

There is nothing quite like a refreshing tropical drink on a hot summer day, complete with a little paper umbrella, of course. This smoothie is full of tropical flavors, probiotics, green veggies, and can be made dairy free with coconut milk and coconut kefir.

- ½ cup plain kefir
- ½ cup frozen mango chunks
- 1 banana, fresh or frozen
- ½ cup fresh or frozen pineapple
- 1 handful spinach or kale (optional)
- 1 cup coconut milk
- 2 cups ice

Blend thoroughly in blender and enjoy!

Sugar-free Lemonade

I use organic citrus whenever I'm baking or juicing. Pesticides reside in the rind and I don't like them in my food or drink. No thank you! I don't want anything other than organic, natural ingredients in my lemonade!

- 10 organic lemons, washed and halved.
- ¾ cup Madhava organic agave
- Water
- Ice

Using either an electric or hand juicer, juice 10 lemons. Remove any seeds and pour juice into a 4-quart pitcher. Add agave and stir to blend with lemon juice. Fill pitcher with water and stir to blend. Fill glasses with ice and pour lemonade over ice.

Sugar-free Strawberry Lemonade

This is a pretty, pink, and refreshing summery drink. I make this for almost every barbecue during the hot summer months. It has just the right amount of tang and sweetness.

- 1 cup washed and hulled strawberries
- 10 lemons
- ¾ cup Madhava organic agave
- Water
- Ice

Place prepared strawberries in blender and blend until liquid, usually 10–15 seconds. Using either an electric or hand juicer, juice 10 lemons. Remove any seeds and pour juice into blender with strawberries. Add agave and blend to mix ingredients. Pour into a 4-quart pitcher and fill pitcher with water. Stir to blend. Fill glasses with ice, and pour lemonade over ice.

ENTREES

Blue Cheese Turkey Burgers

One of my first concerns about going gluten-free was giving up various cheeses. I love blue cheese, Gorgonzola, and other soft cheeses. Some soft cheeses, including some blue cheeses, contain gluten. Please check with the cheese maker to confirm that your cheese is made the old-fashioned way and does not contain gluten.

I prefer turkey to beef because ground turkey is much less fattening than ground beef. I love to add protein to my diet, so I end up grilling turkey burgers all summer long!

- 1½ lbs. ground turkey
- 1 tsp. steak seasoning
- ½ tsp. sea salt
- ¼ tsp. fresh ground black pepper
- 2 oz. blue cheese or other soft cheese
- 4 gluten-free hamburger buns
- Arugula (optional)
- Tomatoes
- Red onion, thinly sliced

Heat grill to medium-high.

In medium bowl, gently fold together ground turkey, steak seasoning, salt, and pepper. Shape mixture into 4 equal sized balls. Make a small indentation in center of each turkey ball. Shape blue cheese into 4 equal-sized flat disks and place a disk in the center of each turkey ball. Wrap turkey around cheese, pinching to seal. Press burgers gently to flatten slightly.

Lightly oil grill. Place burgers on grill and cover. Cook until grill marks are visible on first side, about 5 minutes. Flip burgers and cook until grill marks are visible on the other side and burger is cooked through, 5–7 minutes.

Serve on gluten-free buns or on a bed of arugula. Top with sliced tomato, sliced red onion, and favorite condiments.

Moroccan Lamb Burgers

Fresh ground spices yield much more flavor than prepackaged ground spices. I keep small glass containers of cumin seed, coriander seed, fennel seed, and others. When needed, I roast the seeds in a small skillet with a drop of olive oil until browned. I then use my pestle and mortar to grind exactly what I need. The flavor is vastly different. You won't use prepackaged dried spices once you try this method.

Lamb Burger:

- 2 lbs. ground lamb
- 1 Tbsp. fresh ground cumin
- ½ tsp. cayenne
- Dash of nutmeg
- 1 tsp. ground fennel
- 1 tsp. ground coriander
- Fresh ground black pepper
- ½ tsp. sea salt
- ¼ cup chopped cilantro
- 1 squeeze lemon over fresh chopped cilantro
- ¼ cup chopped mint
- Gluten-free hamburger buns
- Arugula
- Cherry tomatoes chopped in half

Ajvar mayo (roasted red pepper sauce):

- I buy ajvar, a red pepper hummus, at a local specialty foods market and mix it with a natural mayonnaise.
- 1 cup mayonnaise (I use Lemonaise Light)
- 1 (7.25- to 10-oz.) jar roasted red peppers, drained
- 2 cloves garlic
- Sea salt
- ⅛ tsp. fresh ground black pepper
- ½ tsp. white vinegar

Heat grill to medium-high.

In medium bowl, gently fold together ground lamb, cumin, cayenne, nutmeg, fennel, coriander, pepper, sea salt, cilantro, lemon, and mint. Shape mixture into 4 equal-sized burgers.

Lightly oil grill. Place burgers on grill and cover. Cook until grill marks are visible on first side, 4–5 minutes. Turn over and cook until grill marks are visible on the other side and burger is cooked through, another 4–5 minutes. Burgers will still be slightly pink inside for medium-rare burgers.

Serve on gluten-free buns or bed of arugula. Top with halved cherry tomatoes and Ajvar mayo.

Enchiladas

Ancho chili is not spicy. It adds a deep, smoky flavor to dishes and sauces. I use dried chili pods in place of prepackaged dried spices for an even fuller flavor. The main source of heat is the seeds, so I always remove them. You can play with the spice of this dish by adding more as you go if you want more heat. Be sure that you always remove all stems. These enchiladas are delicious served with fresh avocado and a side of black beans.

Blend chilies, chicken stock, dried onion, cumin, and salt in blender until smooth, about 35 seconds to a minute, depending on your blender. you want to see the flecks of chili still visible in the liquid. (You do not want to blend it into a thick paste.)

Pour chili mixture into medium stockpot.

Simmer on medium-low for 15–17 minutes.

- 1.5 oz. California chili pods broken open so you can remove seeds and stems
- ¼ tsp. dried ground Ancho chilis or one Ancho pod with seeds and stem removed
- 3 Anaheim chilies roasted at 400 degrees for 20 minutes, waxy skins peeled off and seeds removed
- 2 cups low-sodium chicken stock (or veggie stock for vegetarian enchiladas)
- ¼ cup dried minced onion
- ½ Tbsp. fresh ground cumin
- ½ tsp. sea salt

Enchiladas (continued)

Chicken Filling:

- 1 whole roasted chicken—I use organic rotisserie chicken from Whole Foods, meat removed and cut into small cubes
- 3 cups shredded cheese
- ½ cup diced green onion
- 1 cup rice (optional)

Vegetarian Filling:

- 1 cup black beans
- 1 cup rice
- 3 cups shredded cheese
- ½ cup diced tomatoes
- ½ cup frozen corn
- ½ cup diced green onion
- 12 corn or other gluten-free tortillas.

Preheat oven to 400 degrees.

Pour ½ cup enchilada sauce into baking dish. Dip tortillas in sauce and fill with filling of choice. Roll tortillas and line up in baking dish. Once dish is filled with enchiladas, cover with remaining sauce and cheese.

Bake at 400 degrees for 10–15 minutes until cheese is nice and bubbly and tortillas have browned. Let sit for 5 minutes to allow enchiladas to set up before serving.

"Spaghetti" and Meatballs

When I decided to change our diet, pasta was the hardest food for me to give up. I love pasta. I love Italy and all Italian food. I needed to find a replacement that would work with all of my sauces and that could fill my pasta cravings. Spaghetti squash is very tasty on it's own, and it transforms into something even more delectable when paired with pasta sauce and these cheesy garlicky meatballs.

Spaghetti:
- 1 large spaghetti squash
- ¼ cup basil
- Parmesan cheese

Meatballs:
- 2 lbs. ground meat (I like 1 lb. each of lamb and bison)
- 4 cloves garlic, minced
- ½ cup chopped fresh basil
- 1 cup grated Pecorino Romano cheese
- 3 Tbsp. gluten-free Italian bread crumbs
- ¼ tsp. crushed red pepper
- 1 tsp. sea salt
- Fresh ground black pepper
- 2 Tbsp. olive oil

Sauce:
- 2 Tbsp. olive oil
- 2–3 cloves garlic, minced
- 1 (28-oz.) can fire-roasted diced tomatoes
- 1 (7-oz.) can tomato paste
- 1 Tbsp. white wine vinegar
- 1 tsp. sea salt
- ¼ tsp. fresh ground black pepper
- 1 Tbsp. Madhava organic agave

Preheat oven to 375 degrees.

Split spaghetti squash in half lengthwise and scoop out seeds. Place on baking dish, cut side down, with 1-inch of water. Roast at 375 degrees for 40–45 min. While spaghetti squash is roasting, form meatballs.

Combine ground meat, minced garlic, chopped basil, Romano cheese, bread crumbs, red pepper, salt, and fresh ground black pepper. Form into 2-inch meatballs. Heat 2 tablespoons olive oil in large skillet over medium-high heat. Brown meatballs in skillet, turning every 2–3 minutes so that meatballs brown evenly and cook through.

Heat olive oil in medium saucepan on medium-high heat. Sauté garlic until lightly browned, 2–3 minutes. Add diced tomatoes, tomato paste, white wine vinegar, sea salt, pepper, and agave. Bring to a boil, reduce heat to low, and simmer for 5 minutes. Pour sauce over meatballs and simmer for 10 minutes.

Once squash is cooked, let cool slightly. Using a large fork, remove "spaghetti" from shell. Add ¼ cup chopped basil to "spaghetti." Plate "spaghetti" and top with meatballs and sauce. Garnish with grated Parmesan cheese and enjoy!

Faux Pasta Chicken Pesto

I love pasta and pesto. In this recipe, I've substituted the pastas for spaghetti squash, creating delectable and nutritious "faux" pasta. I pair it with my Basic Basil Pesto (see page 29) for a dish that your entire family will enjoy!

- 1 large spaghetti squash
- 2 Tbsp. olive oil
- ¼ cup fresh chopped basil
- Sea salt
- Fresh ground black pepper
- 4 boneless, skinless chicken breasts (or you can use extra firm tofu)
- Basic Basil Pesto (see page 29) or your favorite pasta sauce
- Fresh grated Parmesan cheese

To roast squash, preheat oven to 375 degrees. Cut squash lengthwise in half and remove seeds. Place cut side down on roasting pan filled with 1 inch of water. Roast at 375 for 40–45 minutes until a fork can easily be inserted. Let cool slightly. Using large fork, remove squash "spaghetti" into large mixing bowl. Add olive oil, basil, sea salt, and pepper, and toss together. Divide squash equally among four plates.

Marinate chicken in pesto sauce for a minimum of 30 minutes while squash is roasting. Bake, covered, on greased baking dish with sauce marinade at 375 degrees for 20 minutes. Remove cover and bake another 5 minutes until chicken is cooked through and lightly browned. Let chicken cool slightly. Slice chicken diagonally into 1 inch slices and place on top of roasted "spaghetti." Sprinkle with cheese and enjoy!

eat free

Chicken Pot Pie

Nothing says comfort food on a cold night like chicken pot pie. I can't eat traditional pie crust as it's made with wheat flour, but I think this version rivals the best pot pies for flavor and texture.

Crust:
- 2 cups Honeyville blanched almond flour
- ½ cup grated hard cheese (I use Manchego but Parmesan works great too.)
- ½ tsp. sea salt
- 4 Tbsp. unsalted butter, cold and cut into small pieces
- 1 egg

Filling:
- 5 Tbsp. butter, melted
- 1 onion
- 3–4 carrots
- 3–4 potatoes (peeled and cubed) soaked in cold water
- 1 cup mushrooms
- ⅓ cup cognac or brandy (optional—the alcohol cooks out and leaves a great flavor)
- 2 Tbsp. arrowroot powder
- 2¼ cups chicken stock (cold or at room temperature)
- 1 cup milk
- 5 cups chicken (I use organic rotisserie chicken diced into bite-sized pieces)
- 1 cup peas
- 2 Tbsp. parsley
- 2 Tbsp. thyme

Preheat oven to 350 degrees.

Pulse all ingredients for crust in food processor until it forms a ball and set aside.

Melt butter in large stockpot. Add onions and carrots. Drain potatoes and add to stockpot. Cook vegetables until brown, 10–15 minutes. Add mushrooms and cognac or brandy to bring out the flavor of the mushrooms. Cook until mushrooms give up their juice, 3–5 minutes.

In small bowl, whisk together arrowroot powder and ¼ cup chicken stock. Add arrowroot/stock mixture along with remaining chicken stock to stockpot and bring to boil until mixture thickens slightly. Add milk and cook for 2 minutes. Add chicken, peas, parsley, and thyme. Remove stockpot from heat.

Pour filling into ramekins or large baking dish. Break crust into bite-sized pieces to cover top of filling. Bake at 350 degrees for 10–15 minutes until crust is browned.

Cool slightly and enjoy!

rhiannon lawrence

Delicious Tofu and Tomatoes

My sister-in-law Duong is Vietnamese. She has taught me so many wonderful dishes and shared so many incredible flavors with me. This is a variation of a dish that she has made for me. It's very simple and delicious. I enjoy this as a side or as a vegetarian main course.

- 2 Tbsp. grapeseed oil
- 1 (12-oz.) package extra-firm tofu, drained and sliced into 1-inch cubes
- Sea salt
- Fresh ground black pepper
- Garlic powder
- 5 tomatoes, sliced into ¼-inch slices
- 3 cloves garlic, minced

Heat oil in large skillet over medium-high heat and add tofu. Season generously with sea salt, pepper, and garlic powder. Fry tofu until golden brown on all sides, 10–12 minutes. Add garlic and sauté until brown, 1–2 minutes. Add sliced tomatoes and cover with lid, simmering for 10 minutes until tomatoes are softened.

Serve over rice or alone as a side dish.

Fish Sticks

Our kids love fish. In fact, we are all big fish eaters at our house. Sometimes the kids crave an easy, finger friendly dish. Be sure to set everything up before starting so that this recipe can come together quickly. Start with three similar-sized bowls so that you can move the fish from the almond flour to the egg wash to your batter mixture and then right into your skillet!

- 2 eggs
- 1½ cup Honeyville blanched almond flour, divided in half
- 1 tsp. lemon zest
- 1 tsp. finely chopped fresh dill
- ½ tsp. sea salt
- Fresh ground black pepper
- 2 Tbsp. grapeseed oil or butter
- 2 Tbsp. olive oil
- 1 lb. white fish—halibut or cod
- Lemon wedges

In first small bowl, whisk together eggs and set aside. In second small bowl mix half of almond flour, lemon zest, dill, sea salt, and pepper and set aside. In third small bowl place remaining almond flour.

Heat grapeseed oil or butter and olive oil in large skillet over medium-high heat. Cut fish into 1-inch wide pieces. Dip fish pieces into plain almond flour first, then into eggs, and finally into dill-lemon mixture. Fry each piece of fish for about 1–2 minutes per side until cooked but still soft. Let cool slightly on paper towel–lined plate, squeeze fresh lemon onto fish sticks, and serve!

Mexican Lettuce Cups

My family loves Mexican food. We do "Freaky Deaky Taco Tuesday" each week with variations of tacos.
This dish is as colorful as it is flavorful and is very simple to prepare, making it a favorite for everyone!

- 2 Tbsp. olive oil
- ½ red onion, diced
- 4 organic chicken breasts—chopped into bite-sized pieces
- 1 Tbsp. Ancho chili powder
- 2 Tbsp. fresh ground cumin
- 1 tsp. chili powder (more or less depending on desired heat)
- Pinch of cayenne pepper (optional—this will kick up the heat if desired)
- 1 tsp. garlic powder
- 1 tsp. sea salt
- 1 (8-oz.) can black beans, drained
- 1 (14-oz.) can diced fire roasted tomatoes
- 1 cup frozen corn kernels
- Gluten-free tortillas or washed lettuce halves
- Shredded cheese

Heat olive oil in large skillet over medium-high heat and sauté onion until translucent and starting to brown. Add chicken pieces, Ancho chili powder, cumin, chili powder, cayenne pepper (optional), garlic powder, and salt, and cook until chicken is no longer pink. Add black beans, fire-roasted tomatoes with juice, and corn, and stir until everything is heated through.

Fill gluten-free tortillas or washed lettuce halves and top with cheese for a quick and colorful meal.

Parmesan Chicken Strips

This is my version of chicken strips, and my kids devour these. I like to pair them with my Arugula Salad with Lemon Vinaigrette (see page 22) for a more adult version.

- 4 boneless, skinless chicken breasts, washed
- 1¾ cup Honeyville blanched almond flour
- 1 tsp. sea salt
- 3 eggs
- 1 cup grated Parmesan cheese
- ½ tsp. fresh ground black pepper
- ¼ tsp. garlic powder
- ¼ tsp. Italian seasoning: dried oregano, rosemary, thyme, marjoram, and sage
- 2 Tbsp. butter or grapeseed oil
- 2 Tbsp. olive oil

Slice chicken into 1-inch thick strips, pat dry, and set aside.

Set up your workstation so that you have three bowls side by side. In first bowl, mix 1 cup almond flour with 1 teaspoon sea salt. In second bowl, whisk eggs well until yolks lighten in color. In third bowl, mix Parmesan, remaining almond flour, pepper, garlic powder, and Italian seasoning. Heat butter or grapeseed oil and olive oil in large skillet over medium-high heat.

Coat chicken strips, first in almond flour, second in egg wash, and third in cheese mixture. Fry chicken strips, 2–3 minutes per side, in skillet with oil and butter. When cooked through, drain chicken strips on paper towel lined plate before serving.

Shrimp Stir-Fry

I'm always looking for easy and nutritious dinner ideas that pack a punch. With shrimp, tomatoes, and asparagus, this dish is flavorful and light. I'll serve it over brown rice or steamed spinach. Be sure to use gluten-free soy sauce—various sauces can and do contain gluten.

- 2 Tbsp. gluten-free soy sauce
- 1 Tbsp. seasoned rice vinegar
- 1 Tbsp. grated peeled fresh ginger
- 2 Tbsp. sesame seeds
- 2 tsp. grapeseed oil
- 1 lb. asparagus—washed, ends trimmed, and cut into 1-inch pieces
- 4 large tomatoes—washed and sliced into thick slices, about 8 per tomato
- 1 lb. large shrimp—cleaned, deveined, and cooked

Mix together soy sauce, rice vinegar, and ginger, and set aside.

Toast sesame seeds in medium skillet for 2–3 minutes over medium-high heat until lightly browned.

Heat grapeseed oil over medium-high heat, add asparagus, and cook for 5 minutes until crisp-tender. Add tomatoes and cook 2 minutes longer until tomatoes give up juice. Stir in soy sauce mixture. Add cooked shrimp and heat 1 minute longer. Remove from heat and stir in toasted sesame seeds.

Serve over rice.

Spinach and Feta-Stuffed Chicken

My husband loves a little local Greek restaurant and their spinach and feta-stuffed chicken. Instead of the breaded and fried version, I've created a lighter and healthier option that is filled with flavor.

- 1 cup spinach, finely chopped
- ½ cup feta cheese crumbles
- 1 cup mushrooms, finely diced
- ½ cup toasted pine nuts, chopped
- 2 Tbsp. chopped herbs (fresh oregano, mint, or basil)
- Dash of sea salt
- Fresh ground black pepper
- 4 chicken breasts, washed and butterflied
- Olive oil

Preheat oven to 375 degrees.

In a small bowl, combine chopped spinach, feta, mushrooms, toasted pine nuts, herbs, salt, and pepper. On a clean work surface, lay out your four butterflied chicken breasts. Fill each breast with one-fourth of the spinach and feta filling. Roll each filled chicken breast in a spiral and secure with toothpicks. Place chicken breasts in a lightly oiled baking dish and bake at 375 for 25 minutes. Serve hot out of the oven.

Gorgonzola-Stuffed Chicken

Gorgonzola-stuffed chicken is my husband's and son Ben's favorite dish. We make this for special occasions and to impress our friends because it's fast and simple to prepare. Be sure to use gluten-free Gorgonzola cheese made the old-fashioned way through fermentation. Not all soft cheeses are gluten free.

Preheat oven to 375 degrees.

In a small bowl, combine chopped spinach, Gorgonzola cheese crumbles, salt, and pepper. Mix with fork and set aside. In a small skillet, sauté shallot in 1 tablespoon oil until soft, remove from heat, and let cool for 2–3 minutes. Add shallot to spinach-Gorgonzola mix.

On a clean work surface, lay out your four split chicken breasts. Fill each breast with one-fourth of the spinach-Gorgonzola mix. Roll each chicken breast into a spiral and wrap each chicken breast with 1–2 pieces bacon.

Lightly oil baking dish and place stuffed breasts in pan. Bake at 375 degrees for 25 minutes and then turn on broiler and cook for 2–5 more minutes until the bacon is crispy. Remove from oven and enjoy!

- 1 cup spinach, finally chopped
- ½ cup Gorgonzola cheese crumbles
- Dash of sea salt
- Fresh ground black pepper
- 1 large shallot, minced
- 1 Tbsp. olive oil plus extra
- 4 chicken breasts, washed and split
- 4–8 pieces of thin, nitrate-free bacon or pancetta

Stuffed Mushroom Chicken

I've always loved stuffed mushrooms. I make really savory vegetarian-stuffed mushrooms, and one day I thought, "Wouldn't these be delicious in a chicken breast?" I was right. I love this dish over a bed of steamed spinach, and our kids love to eat it over gluten-free pasta.

- 4 boneless, skinless chicken breasts, butterflied
- Canola oil spray or butter for your pan

Filling:

- ½ cup grated Pecorino Romano cheese
- 1 cup chopped mushrooms
- ⅓ cup chopped baby spinach
- 2 Tbsp. chopped Italian parsley
- 2 Tbsp. chopped mint
- 2–3 cloves garlic, chopped
- 2 Tbsp. softened butter
- Sea salt
- Fresh ground black pepper

Preheat oven to 350 degrees.

Add grated Pecorino Romano cheese to chopped mushrooms, spinach, parsley, and mint. Add garlic, softened butter, salt, and pepper, and mix together thoroughly.

On a clean surface, lay out butterflied chicken breasts. Fill each breast with one-fourth mushroom mixture, close up, and secure with toothpicks. Grease a large baking dish with canola oil spray or butter and place chicken breasts in baking dish, filling-side down. Cover dish with foil and bake at 350 degrees for 25–30 minutes.

Teriyaki Salmon

The sauce in this recipe is both a marinade and glaze for salmon, chicken, or tempeh. Salmon is my favorite so I've outlined it here. My family loves salmon so I always double the recipe. I also love tempeh in this marinade. My best friend is vegetarian, so I'm always looking for vegetarian modifications to recipes so that I can feed her when she drops in for dinner. Tempeh by itself can be kind of lackluster and flavorless, but marinated in this teriyaki sauce it is just scrumptious!

- ¾ cup gluten-free soy sauce
- ¾ cup water
- 2–3 cloves garlic, minced
- 3 tsp. fresh ginger, minced
- ¾ cup Madhava organic agave
- 4 salmon fillets
- 1 Tbsp. arrowroot powder mixed with ¼ cup cold water

In a medium saucepan, bring first 5 ingredients to boil over high heat. Boil for 1 minute and remove from heat. Allow sauce to cool before marinating salmon.

Arrange salmon, skin-side up, in a glass baking dish. Pour cooled marinade over salmon. Cover and marinate in refrigerator for 1 hour to overnight. Move salmon to a plate and reserve marinade.

Preheat oven to 375 degrees.

In a medium saucepan, bring arrowroot powder mixture and marinade to boil. Cook until thickened, 2–3 minutes.

Arrange marinated salmon on a foil-lined baking dish, skin-side down. Brush glaze over salmon and bake at 375 degrees for 20–25 minutes, depending on the thickness of salmon fillets. Be careful not to overcook your salmon!

SOUPS

Chicken and Rice Porridge

I make this soup after I've roasted a chicken for enchiladas, pot pie, or any of our other chicken recipes. If you don't have a roasted chicken from another meal, you can use diced chicken. I made a variation of this recipe every week for my daughter for the first year of her life. She loves this porridge. To dress it up for the grown-ups, I add a few drops of Asian chili garlic sauce, some chopped Thai basil, and mint.

- 2 Tbsp. butter
- ½ small onion, diced
- 2 cups cooked rice
- 4 cups chicken stock
- ½ cup carrots, diced
- ½ cup zucchini, peas, corn, or any other veggies you want to add
- ½ cup diced chicken
- Sea salt
- Fresh ground black pepper

Melt butter in medium saucepan.

Add onion and brown for 2–3 minutes or until onion just begins to soften. Add rice and lightly brown. Add chicken stock and bring to a boil. Add veggies and chicken. Reduce heat to medium-low and simmer for 30 minutes. Add salt and pepper to taste.

Chicken Stock

Homemade chicken stock is so much better than what you can find at the store. I like to make this in bulk. It will keep frozen for several months and lasts up to a week in the refrigerator. It's fantastic as a substitute for water in soups and savory entrees.

- 1 lb. chicken parts (neck, wings, and so forth)
- 2 cups chopped celery
- 2 medium carrots, chopped
- 1 large onion, diced
- 5 whole black peppercorns
- 1 tsp. salt
- 4 quarts cold water

In large stockpot, bring chicken, celery, carrots, onion, peppercorns, salt, and water to a boil. Lower heat to medium-low and simmer for 3 hours. Water should barely move. Strain stock, discarding veggies and chicken. Refrigerate stock to separate fat. Fat will collect at the top, making it easy to remove. Yields 14 cups.

Cold Caprese Soup

I love a good caprese salad in the summertime—in fact, it's my favorite meal. With this soup, I wanted to capture the taste of summer in a light cold soup that's easy to make and even easier to enjoy. This dish works great as either an appetizer or main dish along side Parmesan Chicken Strips (see recipe on page 59).

- 2½ lbs. organic tomatoes (heirloom are best, but any will do)
- 2 cloves garlic, chopped
- 1 tsp. salt
- 2 Tbsp. high-grade balsamic vinegar
- ⅓ cup basil, plus a handful for garnish
- 2 cups chicken stock
- 2 Tbsp. high-quality olive oil
- Freshly ground black pepper
- Fresh mozzarella cheese (the kind that is in a ball and stored in liquid)

Combine tomatoes, garlic, salt, balsamic vinegar, and basil in a blender. Blend well for 2–3 minutes until everything is liquefied. Pour tomato mixture into a large pot and mix in chicken stock, olive oil, and freshly ground black pepper. Transfer to serving bowl and chill in refrigerator for a minimum of 1 hour.

Pour into bowls. Add chunks of fresh mozzarella cheese, garnish with chopped basil, and serve.

Roasted Veggie Soup

My family enjoys hearty, warming soups on cold fall and winter evenings.
Manchego and truffle oil make this soup extra decadent!

- 2 lbs total of carrots, parsnips, golden beets, celery root, sweet onion, butternut squash, or sweet potato
- 2 Tbsp. olive oil
- 1 tsp. sea salt
- Fresh ground black pepper
- 1 Tbsp. Madhava organic agave
- 2 cups chicken stock
- 2 Tbsp. chopped fresh herbs (oregano, chives, and Italian parsley are all great)
- Grated Manchego cheese
- Truffle oil for drizzling (optional)

Preheat oven to 375 degrees.

Cut veggies into ½ inch thick slices. In a large bowl, toss veggies with olive oil, salt, pepper, and agave. Transfer to foil-lined baking sheet and bake at 375 degrees for 45 minutes.

After cooling slightly, add veggies and chicken stock to blender and puree. Pour veggie and chicken stock mixture to a large pot and bring to a boil. Reduce heat and simmer for ten minutes. Add fresh herbs.

Sprinkle individual servings with grated Manchego cheese and a few drops truffle oil.

Tomato Fennel Soup

Fennel has many health benefits. Fennel can help anemia, indigestion, and menstrual disorders, just to name a few. This hearty soup contains both fennel bulb and fennel seed.

- 2 Tbsp. good quality olive oil
- 1 medium fennel bulb, trimmed and cored
- 2 Tbsp. feathery fennel leaves for garnish
- 2 large shallots
- 1 medium carrot
- 1 (28-oz.) canned fire roasted tomatoes, undrained
- 2 cups chicken stock
- Sea salt
- Fresh ground black pepper
- 1 Tbsp. roasted fennel seed

Heat oil in medium stockpot over medium heat. Chop fennel, shallots, and carrot into same sized diced pieces and add to stockpot. Cook until soft but not brown, 10–15 minutes. Add tomatoes and broth, bring to boil, reduce heat, and simmer for 15 minutes.

Transfer soup to blender and blend until smooth. Pour back into stockpot and add salt, pepper, and roasted fennel seed and serve.

Southwest Lentil Soup

Lentils are a hearty addition to any soup. They are a great prebiotic, promoting good gut health and adding lots of protein. The spice in this dish is subtle, so you can add more if you like. Spicy, hearty dishes like this one are great for your immune health. Bonus Tip: The leftover soup is delicious can be used as a base for lentil burgers. After a few days, try adding cooked brown rice or gluten-free bread crumbs and form burger patties.

- 2 Tbsp. olive oil
- 2–3 celery stocks, chopped
- 2–3 carrots, chopped
- 1 large onion, diced
- 2 cloves garlic, minced
- 1 cup brown lentils, rinsed and cleaned
- 2 tomatoes, pureed OR 1 (14-oz.) can diced tomatoes
- 1 tsp. sea salt
- ¼ tsp. crushed red pepper
- 4 cups of chicken stock
- 1½ cup water
- 1 tsp. fresh thyme
- Shredded Monterey Jack cheese (try pepper jack if you want more of a kick)
- Fresh avocados, sliced
- Tabasco sauce (optional)

Heat olive oil in stockpot over medium-high heat. Add celery, carrots, onion, and garlic and sauté for 1–2 minutes. Mix in washed lentils, tomato puree, salt, and red pepper. Add chicken stock and water and bring to a boil. Reduce heat to medium-low and simmer, covered, for 20–25 minutes until lentils are tender.

Remove from heat and add fresh thyme. To serve, top with shredded cheese, avocado and a few drops Tabasco.

Vegetable Beef Soup

This is actually two meals in one! I like to make a roast on Little League nights and use the leftovers the next day to make this hearty delicious soup for my family.

Meal 1: Roast

- 1 large organic chuck roast
- Garlic powder
- Sea salt
- Fresh ground black pepper
- Montreal steak seasoning
- 1 large onion
- 1 large stalk celery
- 3–4 garlic cloves
- ½ cup water

Season roast generously with garlic powder, salt, pepper, and Montreal steak seasoning and place in Crock-Pot. Chop up onion, celery, and garlic cloves and add to Crock-Pot. Add water and simmer on low heat for 6–8 hours or until meat is falling apart and very tender. Serve with a nice green salad.

Meal 2: Soup

- Leftover roast and drippings from Meal 1
- 1 (28-oz.) can fire roasted diced tomatoes
- 2 quarts water
- ½ cabbage, chopped into bite-sized pieces

Pour leftover roast, veggies, and drippings from Crock-Pot into stockpot. Add fire roasted diced tomatoes, water, and cabbage. Season with more sea salt, pepper, and garlic salt and simmer over medium-low for 20 minutes.

Vegetable Stock

You can use this tasty vegetable stock in place of chicken stock to make vegetarian versions of my dishes. This vegetable stock will keep in the fridge for about a week or in the freezer for a few months.

- 4 Tbsp. olive oil
- 2 medium onions, chopped
- 2 medium carrots, chopped
- 1 leek, chopped
- 2 celery stocks with leaves, chopped
- 3 medium tomatoes halved
- 6 sprigs of parsley
- 8 black peppercorns
- 1 bay leaf
- 1 tsp. salt
- 4 quarts cold water

In a large stockpot, heat olive oil over medium-high heat. Add veggies and sauté. Cover and simmer for 10 minutes, stirring occasionally.

Add parsley, peppercorns, bay leaf, salt, and water and simmer for 1 hour.

Strain veggies and seasonings through a strainer. Yields 14 cups vegetable stock.

DELECTABLE
DESSERTS

THE HOLY GRAIL OF GLUTEN-FREE, SUGAR-FREE COOKING

Cheesecake with Pecan Crust

I love this cheesecake with fresh strawberry sauce—it's heavenly. It also goes well with sugar-free whipped cream and fresh berries!

Crust:
- 1½ cup frozen pecans (frozen pecans help the melted butter to set up quickly)
- 2 Tbsp. melted butter
- 2 Tbsp. Madhava organic agave

Cheesecake filling:
- 3 (8-oz.) packages cream cheese, softened
- ¾ cup Madhava organic agave
- 3 eggs
- 1 tsp. vanilla

Crust Preparation:

Pulse pecans in food processor until pea sized.

Add butter and agave and blend quickly until ingredients are mixed evenly. Quickly spread dough out into pie pan using fingertips.

Preheat oven to 350 degrees.

Beat cream cheese until smooth. Add agave and mix well. Add eggs, one egg at a time, beating well after each addition. Add vanilla and combine thoroughly. Pour filling into pecan crust, filling to within ½ inch of top of pie pan. Bake at 350 degrees for 25–30 minutes until small cracks appear on top and cheesecake starts to lightly brown.

Let cool and refrigerate until ready to serve.

Chocolate Pretzel Tart

Nothing goes together better than sweet and salty—or, in this case, chocolate and salt. This recipe uses a gluten-free pretzel crust. Feel free to substitute dairy-free milk, if needed. Almond, soy, or coconut milk all work great and will thicken just fine with the arrowroot powder.

Crust:
- 2½ cups gluten-free pretzels
- 6 Tbsp. cold butter, cut into small cubes
- ¼ tsp. powdered Stevia

Filling:
- 3 Tbsp. arrowroot powder
- 1¼ cups whipping cream, with ¼ cup set aside
- 2 cups milk
- ¼ tsp. sea salt
- ½ cup Madhava organic agave
- 2 Tbsp. vanilla
- 1 (10-oz.) package Ghirardelli gourmet 72% cacao baking chocolate

Preheat oven to 350 degrees.

Pulse all ingredients in a food processor to mix until dough forms. Press into a 9-inch pie pan. Bake 350 for 10 minutes or until lightly browned. Cool completely.

Mix arrowroot powder and ¼ cup cream. Bring milk, remaining cream, and salt to a boil. Slowly add arrowroot powder and cream mixture. Whisk until thickened, about 1–2 minutes. Remove from heat and add agave and vanilla. Whisk in chocolate until completely melted.

Let sit for 5 minutes. Pour into pretzel crust and let cool completely. Refrigerate until ready to serve.

Chocolate Raspberry Tort

Raspberries, chocolate, and coffee give this rich dessert it's depth and flavor.

- 2 cups Honeyville blanched almond flour
- ½ cup cocoa powder
- 1½ tsp. baking soda
- ½ tsp. sea salt
- ⅓ cup grapeseed oil
- 1 cup Madhava organic agave
- 2 eggs, lightly beaten
- 1 tsp. vanilla extract
- ½ cup brewed coffee (I use decaf because I love the depth of the flavor but don't need the caffeine)
- 1 cup raspberries, washed and chopped

Preheat oven to 350 degrees.

Prepare a springform pan by oiling and flouring with almond flour.

Sift first 4 ingredients together in a bowl and set aside. Using a hand mixer, or a stand mixer with whisk attachment, mix oil and agave. Add eggs and mix well. Add vanilla, coffee, and dry ingredients, and mix well. Fold in raspberries.

Pour raspberry mixture into prepared springform pan. Bake at 350 degrees for 25–30 minutes or until tester comes out clean when inserted in center of tort.

Let tort cool completely before serving.

rhiannon lawrence

Coconut Cake

Coconut cake is a light and delicious dessert. In the summer, I will top this with fresh berries or my Raspberry Sauce (see page 98) and Easy Sugar-Free Whipped Cream (see page 100).

- 2 cups Honeyville blanched almond flour
- ½ tsp. baking soda
- ½ tsp. sea salt
- ½ cup coconut oil—this may need to be warmed over low heat to liquefy
- ½ cup Madhava organic agave
- 2 eggs
- ½ cup Greek yogurt
- 1 tsp. vanilla

Glaze:
- 1 (13.66- to 14-oz.) can coconut milk
- ¼ cup Madhava organic agave
- 1 Tbsp. arrowroot powder.

Topping Options:
- Easy Sugar-Free Whipped Cream (see page 100); Fresh berries; Raspberry Sauce (see page 99)

Grease and flour 2 9-inch round cake pans or 1 9 x 13-inch cake pan.

Combine almond flour, soda, and sea salt in medium mixing bowl and set aside

Using a stand mixer or hand mixer, combine coconut oil, agave, eggs, Greek yogurt, and vanilla. Pour dry ingredients into wet ingredients and mix well.

Pour batter into prepared cake pan(s). Bake at 350 degrees for 30 minutes or until a toothpick inserted in cake center comes out clean.

While cake is baking, mix all glaze ingredients in a small saucepan, making sure to stir in arrowroot powder before adding heat. Sauce will be lumpy if you add it while warm. Bring glaze to boil until thickened. Remove from heat and let cool.

Once cake has cooled completely, pour coconut glaze over cake. Refrigerate until glaze has set. Top with fresh berries, Easy Sugar-Free Whipped Cream (see page 100), and Raspberry Sauce (see page 98) before serving.

Coffee Cake

My dad makes an amazing coffee cake, but his version isn't gluten free or sugar free. In fact, he puts small toffee bits in it. I don't have a replacement for the toffee, but I still think this cake is divine. I add blueberries, which are a super fruit and full of antioxidants. And, I just love their zing.

- ½ cup grapeseed oil
- ½ cup Madhava organic agave, plus 2 Tbsp.
- 2 eggs
- ½ cup Greek yogurt
- 1 tsp. vanilla
- ½ tsp. soda
- ½ tsp. sea salt
- 2 cups Honeyville blanched almond flour
- 1 tsp. cinnamon, divided in half
- ½ cup blueberries
- 1 (8-oz.) package cream cheese, cut into ½-inch cubes

Preheat oven to 350 degrees and grease and flour an 3-quart oblong baking dish.

Mix together grapeseed oil, agave, and eggs. Add Greek yogurt and vanilla, and mix well. In a separate bowl, mix together soda, salt, almond flour, and ½ tsp. cinnamon. Pour dry ingredients into wet and mix well.

Fold in blueberries and cream cheese chunks. Pour cake batter into oiled and floured cake pan. Mix 2 tablespoons agave with ½ teaspoon cinnamon and drizzle on top of cake. Bake 350 for 20-25 minutes, until a fork inserted in the middle comes out clean.

Holiday Orange Cake

Certain smells and spices remind me of the holidays year round. The smell of cinnamon, cloves, and citrus instantly make me think of Christmas. Be careful when using citrus, and whenever possible, use organic fruit, especially if you're using the rinds of citrus fruit. Chemicals and pesticides reside in the rinds of non-organic fruits and don't belong in your baking. If you can't find organic fruit, be sure to scrub your citrus with a veggie wash before zesting.

- 2 large oranges
- 4 eggs, separated
- ¾ cup Madhava organic agave
- ½ tsp. sea salt
- 1 tsp. baking soda
- 1 tsp. cinnamon
- Pinch of cloves
- 2 cups Honeyville blanched almond flour

Preheat oven to 375 degrees.

Wash oranges with a veggie wash and place in a large pot. Cover oranges with water and boil for 1–1½ hours or until you are able to slide a fork into orange rinds easily. Remove oranges from water and cool completely.

Slice oranges and remove any seeds or inedible parts. Blend oranges in food processor until smooth.

In a small bowl, whip egg whites until stiff peaks form and set aside.

In food processor or blender, add blended oranges, agave, egg yolks, sea salt, baking soda, cinnamon, cloves, and almond flour and blend until smooth. Gently fold in egg whites.

Pour batter into greased 9-inch springform pan. Bake at 375 degrees for 45 minutes until toothpick inserted in the middle comes out clean. Cool cake completely in pan.

Serve alone or with Easy Sugar-Free Whipped Cream (see page 100).

Pumpkin Chocolate Chip Cake

Pumpkin cake always reminds me of fall. My kids and I love to roast pumpkin seeds and eat pumpkin purees.
I think homemade pumpkin puree is just divine—it tastes great and is very nutritious.

- 2½ cup Honeyville blanched almond flour
- 1½ tsp. baking soda
- ½ tsp. sea salt
- 1½ tsp. cinnamon
- 1 tsp. nutmeg
- 1 tsp. cloves
- ¾ cup Madhava organic agave
- ½ cup oil
- 2 eggs
- 1 tsp. vanilla
- 1 cup pumpkin puree
- 1 cup chopped nuts (optional)
- 1 (10-oz.) package Ghirardelli gourmet 72% cacao baking chocolate (optional)
- Cream Cheese Frosting (optional—see page 99)

Preheat oven to 350 degrees and grease and flour 3-quart oblong baking dish.

Mix almond flour, baking soda, salt, cinnamon, nutmeg, and cloves in a medium bowl and set aside.

In a stand mixer, or large mixing bowl using a hand mixer, combine agave, oil, eggs, vanilla, and pumpkin. Mix well.

Slowly add dry ingredients and mix well.

Stir in nuts and/or chocolate chips. Pour cake batter into prepared baking pan and bake at 350 degrees for 25–30 minutes.

Allow cake to cool completely and serve as is or with Cream Cheese Frosting (see page 99).

Pumpkin puree is easy to make. Wash a pie pumpkin and split in half. Scoop out seeds and place split side down on a large baking dish filled with 1 inch water. Bake at 375 degrees for 40–45 minutes. A fork or toothpick should easily slide into pumpkin once it's done. Remove from oven and let cool about 20 minutes until cool enough to handle. Scoop out pumpkin and puree in food processor until smooth, usually 2–3 minutes. Pumpkin puree will keep in the refrigerator for several weeks or in the freezer for several months.

Lemon Rosemary Cookies

I had the most amazing lemon rosemary tea cookies in an Italian coffee shop and am very proud of my gluten-free sugar-free version. I love the light subtle flavors. The almond flour adds extra fiber, protein, and trace minerals, making this a healthy snack for any time of day. And remember, I use organic fruit, especially when I'm using the rind of citrus fruit. Chemicals and pesticides reside in the rind and don't belong in my baking!

- 2 cups Honeyville blanched almond flour
- ¼ tsp. sea salt
- ½ tsp. baking soda
- ⅓ cup Madhava organic agave
- ⅓ cup grapeseed oil
- 1 tsp. vanilla
- 1 Tbsp. chopped fresh rosemary
- 1 Tbsp. lemon zest

Preheat oven to 350 degrees.

Mix almond flour, salt, and soda in a medium mixing bowl and set aside.

Using an electric mixer or wire whisk, combine agave, grapeseed oil, vanilla, rosemary, and lemon zest in small mixing bowl. Pour dry ingredients into wet ingredients using a spatula or wooden spoon.

Drop by spoonfuls onto parchment paper-lined cookie sheet 2–3 inches apart. Bake at 350 degrees for 7–10 minutes until edges are slightly brown.

Let cool completely on cookie sheet to set up before enjoying.

Oatmeal Cookies

- 1½ cup gluten-free oats
- 1 cup Honeyville blanched almond flour
- ½ tsp. sea salt
- 1 tsp. cinnamon
- ⅓ cup grapeseed oil
- ⅓ cup Madhava organic agave
- 1 egg
- 1 Tbsp. vanilla
- ⅓ cup fruit juice sweetened cranberries
- ⅓ cup Ghirardelli gourmet 72% cacao baking chocolate chips
- ⅓ cup pistachios, coarsely chopped

Preheat oven to 350 degrees.

Mix oats, almond flour, salt, and cinnamon in medium mixing bowl and set aside.

In separate medium mixing bowl, whisk together oil, agave, and egg. Add vanilla.

Slowly pour dry ingredients into wet ingredients, mixing well. Stir in cranberries, dark chocolate chips, and pistachios.

Line cookie sheet with Silpat mat or parchment paper. Scoop cookie dough in heaping spoonfuls onto cookie sheet. Bake at 350 degrees for 7–9 minutes until edges are lightly browned.

Cool on pan for 10 minutes before moving to cooling rack.

Orange Chocolate Chip Cookies

Everybody likes a chocolate chip cookie. These are no exception and are a staple at my house. I use big organic oranges for my zest, which adds just the right sweetness! And because I use organic citrus, I don't have to worry about chemicals or pesticides on my orange rinds. The simple, healthy ingredients make these cookies a great energy snack for hiking and other outdoor activities. These have replaced Cliff bars at my house!

- 2 cups Honeyville blanched almond flour
- ½ tsp. sea salt
- ½ tsp. baking soda
- ⅓ cup grapeseed oil
- ⅓ cup Madhava organic agave
- 1 Tbsp. vanilla
- 1 Tbsp. orange zest
- ⅓ cup Ghirardelli gourmet 72% cacao baking chocolate chips

Preheat oven to 350 degrees.

Mix almond flour, salt, and soda in medium mixing bowl and set aside.

Using an electric mixer or wire whisk, combine agave, grapeseed oil, vanilla, and orange zest in a small mixing bowl.

Pour dry ingredients into wet ingredients using a spatula or wooden spoon and mix well. Stir in baking chips. Drop by spoonfuls onto parchment paper-lined cookie sheet 2 inches apart. Bake at 350 degrees for 7–10 minutes until the edges are slightly brown.

Let cool on baking sheet for 10 minutes before moving to wire rack. Cool completely before enjoying.

Peanut Butter Bars

Did your school cafeteria serve peanut butter bars when you were a kid? I love peanut butter and chocolate and wanted a healthy and delicious version of this old school treat. These more than fit the bill!

- ½ cup butter, room temperature
- ¾ cup + ¼ cup Madhava organic agave
- 1 egg
- 1½ cup organic all-natural peanut butter, divided in half
- ½ baking soda
- ½ + ¼ tsp. sea salt
- ¾ cup gluten-free rolled oats
- 1 cup Honeyville blanched almond flour
- 1 tsp. vanilla
- ⅓ cup Ghirardelli gourmet 72% cacao baking chocolate chips

Preheat oven to 350 degrees.

Mix butter, ¾ cup agave, egg, and ¾ cup peanut butter in medium mixing bowl. In separate mixing bowl combine soda, ½ teaspoon sea salt, gluten-free oats, and almond flour.

Add dry ingredients to the wet ingredients and mix well. Press peanut butter mixture into greased cookie sheet and bake at 350 degrees for 15–20 minutes until lightly browned.

In a separate bowl and using an electric mixer, combine remaining agave, peanut butter, sea salt, and vanilla until whipped. Spread topping over warm peanut butter bars. Sprinkle dark chocolate chips over topping and bake for 2 minutes more until chocolate is melted. Spread with spatula to create a thin chocolate layer.

Let bars cool completely before slicing into squares.

Peanut Butter Balls

These easy and fun treats are my version of peanut butter cups. The dark chocolate is a good source of antioxidants and magnesium, and the all-natural peanut butter is full of trace minerals. As a combination of the two, this is one nutritious treat that will please adults and kids alike.

- 1½ cup all-natural peanut butter (the kind with peanuts listed as the only ingredient)
- ¾ cup Madhava organic agave
- ¾ tsp. sea salt
- 1½ tsp. vanilla
- 1 cup Ghirardelli 72% cacao baking chocolate chips

Mix peanut butter, agave, sea salt, and vanilla in small saucepan and bring to a boil. Remove from heat immediately and let cool slightly. Mixture will thicken quickly. Once peanut butter mixture is cool enough to touch, form into 1-inch balls. Set on wax paper and let cool.

While peanut butter balls are cooling, melt chocolate chips in double broiler. I use a glass or metal heat-safe mixing bowl over a small saucepan with a couple inches of boiling water. The chocolate will melt fast. Stir constantly so that the bottom doesn't burn.

Using a spoon, roll peanut butter balls in melted chocolate and set on wax paper. Allow peanut butter balls to set completely before enjoying.

Mocha Almond Cupcakes

These cupcakes remind me of a latte without the caffeine. They are especially delicious with a dollop of sugar-free whipped cream.

- 2 cups Honeyville blanched almond flour
- ¼ cup unsweetened cocoa
- 1 Tbsp. espresso blend decaf coffee
- ½ tsp. sea salt
- ½ tsp. baking soda
- ¾ cup Madhava organic agave
- 2 eggs
- ¼ cup grapeseed oil
- 1 tsp. almond extract
- ½ tsp. vanilla

Preheat oven to 350 degrees.

Mix almond flour, unsweetened cocoa, espresso blend decaf coffee, sea salt, and baking soda in medium mixing bowl. Set aside.

In a separate medium mixing bowl and using an electric mixer or wire whisk, combine agave, eggs, grapeseed oil, almond extract, and vanilla in medium mixing bowl.

Slowly add dry ingredients to wet ingredients, mixing well.

Line a cupcake sheet with paper liners and fill halfway with cupcake batter. Bake at 350 degrees for 18–20 minutes or until a fork comes out clean from the center of a cupcake. Cool completely on a wire rack and top with a dollop of Easy Sugar-Free Whipped Cream (see page 100).

rhiannon lawrence

Red Velvet Cupcakes

At first, coming up with an all-natural, gluten-free, sugar-free adaptation of these classic cupcakes presented a challenge. Traditional red velvet calls for red food coloring. I don't use artificial colorings because I find them toxic. Instead I've used beet puree, which adds a beautiful, deep ruby color and added nutrition.

- 1 Tbsp. + ¼ cup grapeseed oil
- 2–3 medium beets, washed and halved.
- 1¼ cup Honeyville blanched almond flour
- ¼ tsp. salt
- 1 tsp. cocoa powder
- ½ tsp. baking soda
- ½ cup Madhava organic agave
- 1 egg, room temperature
- 1 tsp. vanilla
- ½ cup buttermilk, at room temperature
- ½ tsp. vinegar

Topping Options:
- Cream Cheese Frosting (see page 99); toasted pecan pieces (for decoration)

Preheat oven to 350 degrees.

Grease baking dish with 1 tablespoon grapeseed oil. Wash and halve 2–3 medium beets and place them, cut-side down, onto prepared oiled baking dish. Cover with foil and roast at 350 degrees for 40–50 minutes until fork inserts easily into center of beets. Remove peel. Puree peeled beet halves in a food processor or blender, adding water as necessary if puree is too thick. Allow puree to cool completely before adding to cake mixture.

Sift together almond flour, salt, cocoa powder, and baking soda into small mixing bowl and set aside.

Using an electric mixer or wire whisk, combine agave, ¼ cup grapeseed oil, and egg in large mixing bowl. Add vanilla and ⅓ cup beet puree and mix well. Add buttermilk and vinegar and mix well. Slowly add dry ingredients to wet ingredients, mixing well.

Pour batter into paper-lined cupcake pan, filling each cup half full. Bake at 350 degrees for 12–15 minutes. Cool completely on wire rack and top with Cream Cheese Frosting (see page 99) and toasted pecan pieces. Makes 12 cupcakes.

Basic Vanilla Cupcakes

Greek yogurt is a daily go-to in my house. Yogurt is full of probiotics that are great for immune health, and Greek yogurt is higher in protein than regular yogurt. In this recipe, the Greek yogurt keeps these cupcakes extra moist. These cupcakes are a staple for birthday parties. They are wonderful alone and delicious with a flavored whipped cream or fresh strawberry sauce.

- ½ cup grapeseed oil
- ½ cup Madhava organic agave
- 2 eggs
- ½ cup Greek yogurt
- 1 tsp. vanilla
- ½ tsp. soda
- ½ tsp. salt
- 2 cups Honeyville blanched almond flour

Preheat oven to 350 degrees.

Line a cupcake pan with 12 paper liners OR grease and flour a 9-inch cake pan using almond flour.

In a large bowl and using an electric mixer or wire whisk, mix grapeseed oil, agave, and eggs. Add Greek yogurt and vanilla, and mix well. In separate bowl, mix soda, salt, and almond flour.

Slowly add dry ingredients to wet ingredients, mixing well. Pour batter into lined cupcake pan or prepared cake pan. Bake at 350 degrees for 12–17 minutes for cupcakes or 30–33 minutes for cake or until a toothpick inserted in the middle comes out clean.

Cool completely on a wire rack and top with Strawberry Whipped Cream (see recipe on page 103).

TOPPINGS

Fresh Strawberry Topping

Strawberries are delicious and nutritious: they are rich in antioxidants and vitamins. Strawberries may also help prevent cancer and heart disease. They're the perfect complement to many dishes. This topping is easy and so tasty!

- 1 cup fresh strawberries, washed and sliced
- 2 Tbsp. Madhava organic agave

Blend or process until nice and smooth

Pour over cheesecake, ice cream, or chocolate!

Raspberry Sauce

Raspberries are rich in antioxidants, which help neutralize free radicals in the body and prevent damage to cells. They are vitamin packed and bursting with flavor. I love this topping because I don't use sugar-filled jams and jellies. This is a great topping!

- 1 cup frozen or fresh raspberries
- ⅓ cup water
- ¼ cup Madhava organic agave

In small saucepan, combine all ingredients and bring to a boil.

Cool and serve over coconut cake, vanilla cake, or anything that needs a raspberry topping!

Cream Cheese Frosting

Cream cheese frosting is my favorite topping for cakes and cupcakes. I created this sugar-free version to have as a decadent treat with my desserts. Agave is a low glycemic natural sweetener and is used in place of sugar. Agave is a liquid, so the frosting will need to be chilled to set up.

- 2 (8-oz.) packages cream cheese, room temperature
- ½ cup butter, room temperature
- ¾ cup Madhava organic agave
- 1 tsp. vanilla

In medium bowl, cream together cream cheese and butter until nice and smooth.

Mix in vanilla and agave. Frosting will be a bit runny.

Chill frosting in fridge until it sets up a little more. Use to frost cake or cupcakes and enjoy!

Store remaining frosting in refrigerator, along with anything frosted with cream cheese frosting.

Easy Sugar-Free Whipped Cream (with Stevia)

This is my version of whipped cream. I love it on pies, cakes, cupcakes, and all by itself. It's delicious and completely sugar free!

Whip cream using electric mixer until stiff peaks form.

Add vanilla and stevia and combine.

- 1 pint whipping cream
- ¼ tsp. powdered stevia or a few drops of liquid stevia to taste
- 1 tsp. vanilla

Chocolate Whipped Cream

This is a light, chocolaty alternative for cakes and cupcakes. I love this with
Basic Vanilla Cupcakes (see page 93). Delicious!

- 1 pint whipping cream
- ¼ tsp. powdered stevia or a few drops of liquid stevia to taste
- 1 tsp. vanilla
- 1 tsp. unsweetened cocoa powder

Whip cream using electric mixer until stiff peaks form.

Add vanilla, chocolate, and stevia and combine.

Orange Whipped Cream

I wanted to create a creamsicle flavored dessert for a child's birthday party. This topping paired with my Basic Vanilla Cupcakes (see page 93) does the trick!

- 1 pint whipping cream
- 1 tsp. vanilla
- 1 Tbsp. orange rind
- ¼ tsp. powdered stevia or a few drops of liquid stevia to taste

Whip cream using electric mixer until stiff peaks form.

Add vanilla, orange rind, and stevia and combine.

Strawberry Whipped cream

My daughter loves the color pink. She also loves strawberries. For her second birthday, I wanted to make strawberry shortcake cupcakes. I paired this topping with my basic vanilla cupcakes, and it was a huge hit!

- 1 pint whipping cream
-
- 1 tsp. vanilla
- ½ tsp. natural red food coloring (made from beets)
- ¼ tsp. powdered stevia or a few drops of liquid stevia to taste
- 1 cup finely chopped washed strawberries

Whip cream using electric mixer until stiff peaks form.

Add vanilla, food coloring, and stevia and combine.

Fold in strawberries.

Rhiannon discovered that she was gluten intolerant and pre-diabetic in September 2009. She immediately dove into the world of gluten-free baking and cooking.

Rhiannon works with several non-profit organizations and is an advocate for health and nutrition. She lives with her husband, three children, and hiking companion, Lola the boxer dog, in Bountiful, Utah.

You can follow Rhiannon's musings and creations at www.rhi-created.com.

about the author